CAREERS WITHOUT COLLEGE

HEALTH CARE

by Susan Gordon and Kristin Hohenadel

Series developed by Peggy Schmidt

Peterson's

Princeton, New Jersey

A New Century Communications Book

Other titles in
this series include:

CARS
COMPUTERS
FASHION
FITNESS
MUSIC

Copyright © 1992 by Peggy Schmidt

Gordon, Susan.
    Health care / Susan Gordon, Kristen Hohenadel.
       p.   cm.—(Careers without college)
    ISBN 1-56079-222-1 (pbk.) : $7.95
    1. Allied health personnel—Vocational guidance.
I. Hohenadel, Kristen, 1964– . II. Title. III. Series.
R697.A4G67   1992
610'.69—dc20   92-29557
                                 CIP

Art direction: Linda Huber
Cover and interior design: Greg Wozney Design, Inc.
Cover photo: Bryce Flynn Photography
Composition: Bookworks Plus
Printed in the United States of America
10 9 8 7 6 5

Text Photo Credits
Color photo graphics: J. Gerard Smith Photography
Page viii: © Steve Fenn/ABC
Page xiii, Joan Parsons: © Creative Imagery, Inc.
Page xiv: © Joel Gordon Photography
Page 16: © Woodfin Camp & Associates, Inc./Michal Heron
Page 34: © Reuters/Bettmann
Page 54: © Woodfin Camp & Associates, Inc./Robert Frerck
Page 74: © Woodfin Camp & Associates, Inc./Sepp Seitz

ABOUT THIS SERIES

Careers without College is designed to help those who don't have a four-year college degree (and don't plan on getting one any time soon) find a career that fits their interests, talents and personalities. It's for you if you're about to choose your career—or if you're planning to change careers and don't want to invest a lot of time or money in more education or training, at least not right at the start.

Some of the jobs featured do require an associate degree; others only require on-the-job training that may take a year, some months or only a few weeks. In today's real world, with its increasingly competitive job market, you may want to eventually consider getting a two- or maybe a four-year college degree in order to move up in the world.

Careers without College has up-to-date information that comes from extensive interviews with experts in each field. It's fresh, it's exciting, and it's easy to read. Plus, each book gives you something unique: an insider's look at the featured jobs through interviews with people who work in them now.

Peggy Schmidt

ACKNOWLEDGMENTS

Special thanks to the following people for their contributions to this book:

Don Balasa, Executive Director, American Association of Medical Assistants, Chicago, Illinois

Alan Bode, RT(R), Radiographer Program Director, Abbott Northwestern Hospital, Minneapolis, Minnesota

Cecelia Byrd, Staff Assistant for the Department of Practice, Economics and Policy, American Nurses Association, Washington, DC

Alana Calfee, Director of Certification, Foundation for Hospice and Home Care, Washington, DC

Sergeant Paul Cervantez, Chief Wardmaster, 41st Combat Support Hospital, Fort Sam Houston, Texas

Terri Christensen, Command Information Officer, Fort Sam Houston, Texas

Mike Cogswell, RT(T), RT Temps, Devon, Pennsylvania

Jill Hodge, Research Associate, National League for Nursing, New York, New York

Carol J. Honaker, RNC, Director, Accreditation, Training and Support Services Branch, Division of Home-Based Services, Alabama Department of Public Health, Montgomery, Alabama

Gwen Jensen, Clinical Nurse Specialist, UCLA Medical Center, Los Angeles, California

David Kesterson, Director, National Federation of Licensed Practical Nursing, Raleigh, North Carolina

Deborah Kroll, Council Director of Practical Nursing Programs, National League for Nursing, New York, New York

Nancy Linn, RN, Nurse Recruiter, CIGNA Healthplan of California, Glendale, California

Charity Matic, RN, Clinical Nursing Supervisor, CIGNA Healthplan of California, Arcadia, California

Sherry Pickle, Staff Development Coordinator, Medical Home Health Inc., Sallisaw, Oklahoma

Denise Rolleri, RT(T), President, RT Temps Inc., Devon, Pennsylvania

Anna Soucy, RN, LSW, Longterm Care Coordinator, Visiting Nurses of Aroostook, Fort Kent, Maine

Judi Van Vleet, Assistant Professor of Nursing, Weber State University, Ogden, Utah

John Word, LPN, Executive Director, National Association for Practical Nursing Education and Service (NAPNES), Silver Spring, Maryland

WHAT'S IN THIS BOOK

WHY THESE HEALTH CARE CAREERS?

Doctors and nurses are often the most visible players in the medical arena. But like the behind-the-scenes staff who make theatrical productions possible, it is the army of aides, assistants and technicians that makes our health care system function. Their contributions, whether it's taking an X-ray, wheeling a patient into surgery or drawing blood, are vital ones.

In this book you will read about five health care careers:

❑ Nursing assistant

❑ Home health aide

❑ Licensed practical nurse

❑ Radiologic technologist

❑ Medical assistant

These jobs were chosen because they are the five fastest-growing health care careers that require no more than a two-year degree. They are jobs for people who like people and want one-on-one contact with patients. There is a huge demand for workers in these fields right now, and that demand is expected to keep rising dramatically over the next decade. That's because the health care industry is expected to expand to meet the needs of a growing and aging population.

The good news for young people and career changers is

that it doesn't have to take long to get your foot in the door. If you want to work as a home health aide or as a nursing assistant, you can be trained on the job within a matter of weeks. You can also get a good introduction to the basics of these jobs by taking a vocational health care class at a high school (or the adult education classes at a high school).

Training to become a licensed practical nurse usually takes a year. Medical assisting programs are one or two years in length. You'll need the most education—two years—to become a radiologic technologist.

Before you read about each of these careers, find out what Dr. Nancy Snyderman, a surgeon, has to say about the importance of being part of the medical team. And discover why two veterans of careers featured in this book have found such great satisfaction in their work in the section "Why They Love What They Do."

DR. NANCY SNYDERMAN

on the Rewards of Being Part of the Medical Team

Nancy Snyderman, M.D., is a head and neck cancer surgeon at the University of California Medical Center in San Francisco. But she's more widely known to the public as ABC's "Good Morning America" health and medical expert. Since 1987 she has appeared on the program weekly. She also fills in for Joan Lunden when the "Good Morning America" co-host is on vacation. In addition, Dr. Snyderman appears on the local San Francisco-area ABC evening news five nights a week with updates from the medical world. When she's not on TV, she's doing what she loves most: being a surgeon.

Dr. Snyderman grew up in a family of physicians in Fort Wayne, Indiana. She talks about how she got started in health care and the rewards of working as a member of the medical team.

Health care is one of the few fields where you can genuinely make a difference. I firmly believe that we are put on this earth to leave it a little bit better than we found it, and working in health care is one of the ways you can do that.

I always knew I wanted to be a doctor. My grandfather and my father were both doctors. I remember that my father was always happy with his profession and really enthusiastic about it. He also made the point that it was important to be your own boss. When you're a doctor, you can't get fired by a corporation. You can always hang up the shingle, you can always make a living, you can always put food on the table. It's that sense of independence that led me into medicine. But I also remember how much my father was moved when patients would thank him for helping them. The idea of really helping others, as silly as it sounds to some people these days, really mattered to me.

I didn't spend a lot of time in hospitals trying to find out if I would like working in medicine. I just always knew. But I had one summer job as a respiratory therapist (a specialist who treats patients with heart-lung problems that may interfere with breathing), and that gave me the exposure to what it was like to be in the hospital every day. Nowadays, that job requires specialized education, but back in the '70s I got on-the-job training for it.

I went to medical school at the University of Nebraska. If I hadn't gotten into medical school, I would have found something else to do in medicine. Even when medical school got a little boring I never thought of giving up. I knew that even the parts I hated were temporary, a necessary part of getting through to what I wanted to do. There was always a lot I enjoyed, and once I was able to apply the common sense stuff, where you're out there using what you've learned, it was even more fun.

I started off planning to be a pediatrician, but after beginning to specialize in pediatrics, I began to feel I was really better suited for something else and switched specialties to ear, nose and throat (ENT). I discovered that I have a surgeon's personality, a real Type A personality. I like things done fast. I like instant results. I like the independence of being in the operating room and making decisions. It's very exciting. There's no feeling that I think is as thrilling as being in the OR.

It was in the OR that I got into television. One day during my residency at the University of Pittsburgh, I was doing a tonsillectomy; a camera crew came through doing a news story, and I ended up being interviewed. At the end they said, "Have you ever considered being on television? You might think about it." So I did. I moved to Little Rock, Arkansas, for my first real job as a surgeon at the University of Arkansas, and at the same time, I started in television doing a health segment on the local news for $37.50 per segment. I got discovered by an agent who pitched me to ABC, and I've been at "Good Morning America" since 1987. I do about one segment a week for the show, and I fill in for Joan Lunden eight weeks out of the year.

To keep up with medical news I read a lot. There's no secret to it. It just requires a lot of diligence and a lot of curiosity. I read throwaway medical journals as well as the real medical journals. And I have a computer that's punched into the wire services so I always know what's going on around the world.

My greatest sense of accomplishment comes from medicine, not from television, though. It's the little, most personal moments when you can say, "I did a good job today." Or when someone in a patient's family grabs your hand and says, "Thank you, Dr. Snyderman. You saved my mother and we got another 15 years together, and it's been wonderful." Some of the most memorable times have been when children I've taken care of have brought me drawings. Or when I've gone to the waiting room and told a family waiting there with a bouquet of flowers that their loved one just made it through an operation. They didn't know if they were going to get good news or bad news, but they came with flowers for me nonetheless. That's the kind of stuff that really touches you. Anybody who goes into health care today will be touched by those kinds of things as part of the health care team.

Health care today truly requires a team approach—there's no way you can take care of a patient without that. My life is very much affected by everyone, from the orderlies who bring the patients to the operating room, to the volunteers in the recovery room, to the LPNs who help on the floor. It requires a lot more than just a doctor and an RN—from a respiratory therapist to the people who do the laundry, from the people who take care of the computer system to the people who assist the pharmacist. The hospital is such a fine, oiled machine; it requires so many people with so many different skills and educational levels.

You don't need a four-year degree to be part of that. What makes a difference is enjoying what you do for a living. If you like what you do at work, you're ahead of the game, and everything else falls into place. Often people operating the "machine" feel invisible, and I think a lot of workers do get overlooked. That happens whether you're talking about a hospital or a corporation—or a news station. It's imperative for the people who are on the upper rungs to recognize a job well done by others.

To be successful, though, you have to believe in yourself, and you have to be determined. There are times when things won't make any sense, and you have to believe deep down inside that it's a temporary problem. Skill and talent and smarts are important, but boy, they aren't the magic stuff. The magic stuff is believing in yourself, having a good work ethic and not letting anything stand in the way of reaching your goal. Now what makes life fun, if you combine all that, is never losing your curiosity. As adults we sometimes turn that off. If you can recapture that curiosity that kids have, you get to enjoy yourself on top of everything.

There are so many new developments ahead of us in health care, and technology is going to continue to grow in importance. Look, for example, at genetic engineering and the work being done in mapping out the human chromosome: the options are just unbelievable. We're going to start curing more diseases with medicine and stop doing so much surgery. I think the most interesting thing we can look forward to is being able to take a blood test to find out if we're predisposed to certain cancers and then being able to change our life accordingly so we won't get them. That's going to be very possible. It's going to be a very exciting next couple of decades.

The field of health care is exciting and challenging at every level. It's always changing, always advancing. It is the most dynamic part of our culture, when you think of the changes that have taken place in the last twenty years. Some of the most important moral and ethical decisions we must make in our society have to do with health care— issues such as ''test tube babies'' and suicides by the terminally ill. These are manifestations of the role technology now has in our lives. To be involved in all this is very, very exciting. And if you're part of the medical team, you will be on the front line.

WHY THEY LOVE WHAT THEY DO

The careers in this book may not be as glamorous as Dr. Snyderman's, but many who work in health care stay in it for life and find satisfaction and pride in their work. Below are sketches of two women who love their professions and have had long, successful careers.

Joan Parsons, Radiologic Technologist and Director, Medical Imaging Education, American Society of Radiologic Technologists (ASRT)

Hattie O'Bryant, Licensed Practical Nurse and President, National Association for Practical Nurse Education and Service (NAPNES)

Though O'Bryant, 60, calls licensed practical nursing (LPN) "the first rung on the career ladder of the nursing profession," she chose not to go on to become a registered nurse (RN). "I stopped at LPN because I enjoyed bedside nursing and felt that this was what I really wanted to do."

For the past 30 years O'Bryant has worked as an office nurse at a private OB/GYN practice in Macon, Georgia, and has been extremely active in practical nursing organizations. She's currently serving her second term as the president of NAPNES. Over the years she has fought for and won increased professional recognition and higher salaries for LPNs.

Though O'Bryant could have advanced her career and increased her salary by going on for her RN, as she encourages young LPNs to do, she has found for herself that "money isn't everything. It's the satisfaction you get when you help a person."

Parsons, 50, came from a single-parent family and needed to work, so she enrolled in one of the first two-year education programs in radiologic technology. She later became the first technologist to get further education in the field of nuclear medicine technology at Aultman Hospital, in Canton, Ohio.

Parsons has had many jobs in her field, in hands-on technology as well as in education and administration. "I've always liked to serve people," she says, "and on top of that, I've always liked to be in charge. This profession has allowed me to do both."

Parsons has also held many offices in associations for radiologic technology. Her greatest honor, she says, was being elected president of ASRT.

Parsons recently became an executive at ASRT. As the director of medical imaging, she develops continuing education programs for the national membership. "I really feel right now that I'm in a different phase of my career," she says. "I have served patients, I have served students and now I'm serving the profession."

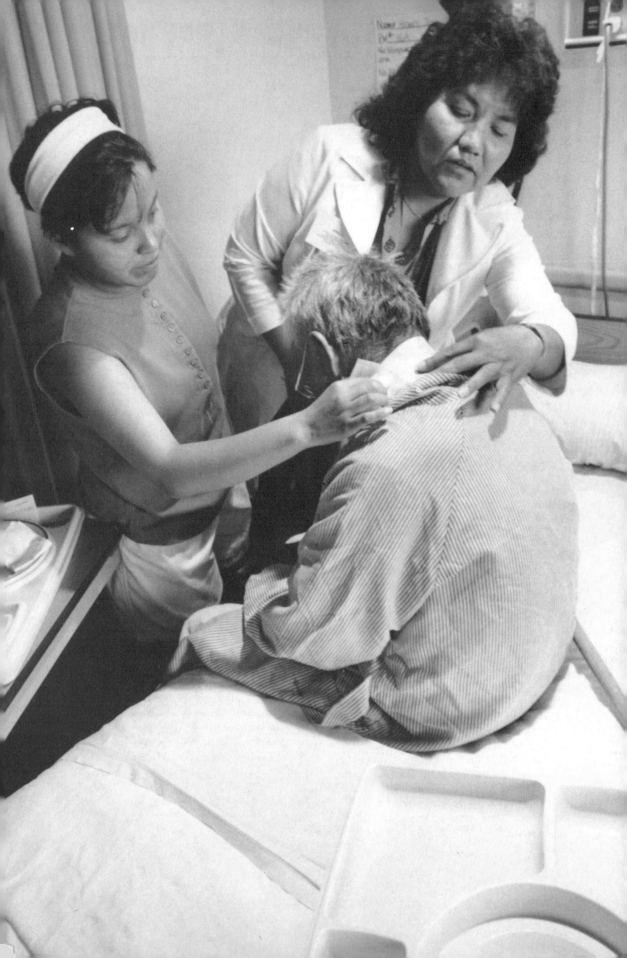

NURSING ASSISTANT

Handwritten note:

NA's CNAs do the hands on work of bathing, feeding, and giving medication to patients making it possible for Nurses & doc. to spend more time on the technical & admin. aspects of their jobs.

Handwritten note:

Nursing Assistants can be life savers. its often up to them to communicate vital info. about a patients medical condition to their supervisors—this can make the diff in life & Death (pg. 1 NA)

"... es?"

Wit ... ing as-

sist ... egin

the... ember of

t ... who pro-

v ... ake all

t ... erceives

t ... alth care

fa ...

... be life

... municate

... medical

... his can

... make the difference between life and death.

Nursing assistants (NAs) and certified nursing assistants (CNAs), who are also referred to as nurses' aides and orderlies, do the hands-on work of bathing, feeding and giving medication to patients, making it possible for nurses and doctors to spend more time on the technical and administrative aspects of their jobs.

Whether you work in a nursing home or a hospital, on a typical day you will assist w'th ___ivering meals, making beds and answering cal'' ___ help a registered nurse (RN) cha___ ___ ___ a wound, go on supply ___ ___ ___ home, assistants usually ___ ___ a licensed practical nurs ___ ___ urse (LVN).

You can tra ___ ___ ___ing assistant or take courses t___ ___ it. Either way, you can break into ___

Many nursing ass___ ___ of the relationships they form with th___ ___ a patient is having a bad day or is ov___ ___ or confused, he or she may behave badly ___ unkind even though they know you are the___ ___ Similarly, the nurses and doctors you work ___ ___ es allow the stress of their jobs to get to them a___ ___ make curt demands or act as if your role is unimportant. You must have the self-confidence to know that your job is critical even when patients or other members of the medical staff don't appreciate it as much as they should.

You can, however, love the work if you are someone who gets great satisfaction from taking care of others and knowing you can help them feel more comfortable.

What You Need to Know

❑ Basic physiology (how the muscles, nerves, body systems function)

❑ How aging can affect mental and physical functioning

❑ Medical terms (so you can comfortably talk with other members of the medical team)

Necessary Skills

❑ Good note-taking (ability to write down information accurately on patients' charts)

❑ Ability to clearly communicate information to other members of the medical team

❑ Be able to give bed baths, transfer patients from their beds to a gurney (a stretcher on wheels) and turn patients who cannot move themselves in their bed

❑ Know how to feed patients who may have difficulty chewing and swallowing food

❑ Good powers of observation to recognize changes in patients' medical condition

❑ Be able to take vital signs (pulse rate, breathing rate, blood pressure, temperature)

Do You Have What It Takes?

❑ Self-confidence and ability not to take personally criticism or shortness from other members of medical team

❑ A sympathetic ear

❑ Patience (sick and elderly patients in poor health can be extremely demanding)

❑ A real desire to help sick or elderly people feel better and more comfortable

❑ Ability to get along with, talk to and comfort different kinds of people

❑ A positive, upbeat attitude

❑ Ability to show up on time (many people depend on your being prompt)

◆ **Getting into the Field**

3

❑ Self-control (you cannot lose your temper when you think patients are mistreating you)

Physical Attributes

❑ Good health (the work is physically demanding and draining)
❑ A strong back and good upper-body strength (you will have to lift and turn patients too weak to move themselves)
❑ A clean, neat personal appearance and good hygiene

Education

A high school diploma recommended but not necessary.

Licenses Required

No states require licenses, but nursing assistants who apply to work in nursing homes must earn a certificate. In 1992 the federal government issued guidelines to raise the level of training for these nursing assistants to 75 hours of instruction and clinical work. Some states, for example, Florida, also require nursing assistants to pass a written and practical exam to become registered with the state. Check with your State Board of Nursing to find out about requirements in your state. You can find the agency listed in your telephone book under state government agencies.

Job Outlook

Job openings will grow: much faster than average
The job of a nursing assistant is one of the fastest growing of all occupations tracked by the federal government. It is projected that by the year 2005, the number of nursing assistants will grow by 43.4 percent, from 12,740 in 1992 to 18,260 in 2005.

The Ground Floor

Entry-level job: nursing assistant (women are sometimes called nurses' aides and men, orderlies)

While the job description is the same for beginners and experienced nursing assistants, in some institutions experienced assistants have more independence or handle more procedures. A nursing assistant who wants more responsibility must go back to school and get more training in another health-related career.

Beginners and Experienced Nursing Assistants

❏ Bathe patients who cannot do so themselves
❏ Help feed patients
❏ Help patients with bodily necessities and personal hygiene (for example, take them to the bathroom, change bedpans, help them brush their teeth)
❏ Turn, position and transfer patients from beds to wheelchairs and gurneys and to and from treatment areas
❏ Observe and report abnormal symptoms (such as blood in the urine or stool)
❏ Talk to patients (about how they're feeling, mentally and physically)
❏ Improve patients' surroundings, make them comfortable
❏ Write down how much food patients eat, liquids they drink and when they go to the bathroom

In nursing homes most nursing assistants work a 40-hour week, with the most common shifts from 7 A.M. to 3 P.M., 3 P.M. to 11 P.M. and 11 P.M. to 7 A.M. In hospitals the shifts may run longer, up to 10 or 12 hours. In your first few jobs you will probably not have a choice of hours and may have to work the late-night shift. Overtime is sometimes available. You may be required to be on call. There are many possibilities for part-time and temporary work.

Usually nursing assistants get two weeks of paid vacation per year and get a certain number of major holidays off (everyone has to take their turn working on these days). In a hospital there are somewhat fewer patients during major holidays, making it more likely for you to get the holiday off that you request. However, in a nursing home, where patients live year round, it's harder to get most major holidays off.

Who's Hiring

❑ Nursing homes (they offer the greatest number of openings)
❑ Hospitals
❑ Registries (agencies that place the nursing assistants who work for them on temporary or long-term assignments)

On-the-Job Hazards

❑ Slips, trips and falls (caused by water on the floor or accidents by patients who have trouble controlling their bladders)
❑ Exposure to infectious blood, bodily fluid or airborne viruses and diseases (it's essential to follow safety precautions)
❑ Back injuries caused by lifting

Nursing assistants are not required to be immunized against hepatitis, but it is a good idea.

Surroundings

Because nursing homes vary widely in appearance and condition, you should visit and compare several. Some are rundown and dreary, while newer ones have attractive artwork, warm wall colors and pretty curtains. Your work will take you in and out of patients' rooms and lounge areas.

In a hospital you will generally report to the central nurses' station and will not have a desk or your own personal space. You will probably have access to a locker room, where you can store personal belongings, and to an employee lounge, where you can take breaks.

Salaries start at minimum wage ($4.35 per hour) and, depending on where you live, may rise to as much as $10 per hour. Hospitals generally pay more than do nursing homes. Salaries also vary from state to state according to cost of living, but experienced nursing assistants are paid more.

Dollars and Cents

Pay raises and promotions are minimal for nursing assistants, so those who want to move up return to school for further training. Many nursing assistants become LPNs, RNs or medical assistants.

Moving Up

Jobs can be found wherever hospitals and nursing homes are located. States with a large elderly population, such as California, Florida, Arizona, New York and Texas, have many nursing homes and employ large numbers of nursing assistants. In rural areas people tend to stay in their positions longer. In large urban areas the turnover is greater and openings occur more frequently.

Where the Jobs Are

Many vocational high schools, community colleges (no GED or diploma required), American Red Cross offices and even some nursing schools offer training programs for nursing assistants. Costs vary, as do the length of the programs. Many nursing homes offer their own on-the-job training and certification programs.

Training

To find out where to get training that will prepare you to pass the test to become state registered (to work in a nursing home), contact the Board of Nursing or the Department of Education in your state. (Check the phone book under state government listings.)

If you go through a state-approved program and begin working for a nursing home within 12 months of becoming registered, the federal government will reimburse you for the cost of your training through its Medicare/Medicaid program.

The Male/Female Equation

Making Your Decision: What to Consider

While this job is open to both men and women, about 95 percent of all nursing assistants are female. Male nursing assistants usually have an easier time with heavy lifting and the physically challenging elements of the job.

The Bad News
- ❑ Low pay
- ❑ Physically and mentally taxing work
- ❑ Health hazards
- ❑ Little potential to move up
- ❑ Limited recognition and respect by some members of the medical team

The Good News
- ❑ Quick training and entry into the work force
- ❑ Job openings are plentiful
- ❑ Temporary part-time work options
- ❑ Good way to find out if you want to pursue a health care position that requires more education
- ❑ Gratitude of satisfied patients and their families

Tonya Dykes, 26,
certified nursing assistant,
Oakhurst Manor Nursing Home,
Ocala, Florida
Years in the job: five

What do you currently do?

I work at a nursing home tending to the residents' basic
needs—feeding, bathing, showering, making sure they
don't get hurt, keeping them clean and happy. I assist
nurses with dressing bedsores and with whatever else they
need done. I don't do blood work or take vital signs. My
workday starts at 6:45 A.M. and ends at 3:15 P.M. I usually
work for three or four days, have two days off, then start
again.

How did you get started as a nursing assistant?

I went through training in a vocational program during high
school, and my first job after graduating was as a nursing
assistant in Michigan, working 11 P.M. to 7 A.M. At first the
work was kind of scary because I was more or less on my
own—I wasn't training with anybody, my instructors
weren't with me. I worked there a year and a half, then
moved to Florida. It took a while for me to get recertified

9

for this state, but when I did, I worked at Ocala Health Center for a year and a half before coming to Oakhurst Manor. Ocala is one of the biggest retirement spots in Florida. At Oakhurst Manor we have about 120 residents. It's very pretty here—we've just had a remodeling.

What was the hardest part of working in this field during the first few years?
My first death was kind of a shocker. We made rounds at about 4:00 in the morning and returned again at 5:30 A.M. It was wintertime in Michigan, and she was the type of person who liked to have the covers up over her mouth to keep her warm. When we pulled the covers back and we heard that last breath of air coming from underneath the covers, it was really a surprise. But what really got me was being left alone in the room with her. Even though I knew she was gone, her body was still there, and it gave me an eery feeling. You shouldn't get attached to your residents, because it is heartbreaking when they do pass away.

What do you like most about your job?
To see the residents' smiling faces when I walk in every day and say "Good morning" to them and they say "Good morning" to me. People who may not have family say "Thank you" for doing the littlest thing, even just getting them a tissue.

What do you like least about your job?
Being physically abused. When residents have dementia (they are not well mentally) or Alzheimer's (they may not remember who you are), they don't always realize what they're doing and they fight you. I've been slapped, bit, spit on, hit and kicked. You have to keep telling yourself that these residents can't always control their behavior, and that you have to protect them and yourself from harm. A lot of people don't understand how I can do what I do, but it's part of the job. You've got to be very strong on the inside, to keep yourself from fighting back.

What are you most proud of?
Helping someone who's in a very confused and withdrawn state smile and come out of it. Trying to cheer them up and talking to them every day can make them feel good again, and that makes me feel good.

What do you plan to be doing in five years?
I might go on to college to further my education in nursing, possibly to become a registered nurse or an emergency medical technician, riding around in an ambulance.

What advice can you give someone thinking of going into this field?
I would have to say: Take the time to volunteer at a nursing home, to absorb the atmosphere and to find out what a certified nursing assistant really does before you decide to do it. You may find that once you get into this kind of work, you can't or don't want to do it.

Kahlil Tanner, 29,
certified nursing assistant,
UCLA Medical Center,
Los Angeles, California
Years in the job: four

What do you currently do?
I work on what's called the "float team" at UCLA Medical Center, so I go all over the hospital. Every day is different. I take vital signs, bathe patients and provide other basic care. I work a 12-hour shift, from 7 A.M. to 7 P.M., up to five days per week. When I need the money, I do overtime. I've learned to test for blood in urine and in feces, and I've been able to assist doctors with other medical procedures, something I never would have experienced in a nursing home. The doctors and nurses explain things to me as they go along.

How did you get started as a nursing assistant?
I saw an ad in the paper for an opening at a convalescent home in Oregon City. Initially I didn't like the smell of the home, but I got used to it after I trained and worked there. Then I went to a registry (an agency that places nursing assistants) and worked in different homes in the Portland metropolitan area for another four months. When I moved to Los Angeles, I continued to work for the registry a while, as well as at a mental hospital in Westwood, before finding a full-time job. I found working at a hospital to be

a lot easier than working in a nursing home, where there's always something to do. In the hospital you'll have busy days too, but then it'll be slow.

What do you like most about your job?
Helping sick patients get well, seeing them come in and progress and become healthy again. I get a lot of personal satisfaction and enjoyment out of working with people—I just care about people, period.

What do you like least?
Changing bedpans. But it comes with the territory.

What was the hardest part of working in this field at first?
When I was less experienced, taking patients' vital signs was hard. Also, I tried not to get too involved with patients—and I still try not to now. Getting emotionally attached to them can really drain you because not every patient is going to make it. I don't allow myself to get depressed—I have feelings, but I control them.

What do you hope to be doing in five years?
I don't plan to continue as a nursing assistant for very much longer. It was really something I fell into. However, I would like to continue to do volunteer work, and I've always thought about opening a convalescent home. In some convalescent homes you find neglect because there isn't enough manpower, and that's depressing. I'd like to make a lot of changes.

What are you most proud of?
Helping people. I've had patients who have told me I did a lot for them mentally and physically, but mostly mentally. I tell them to stay positive. It's not like I automatically know what to say—sometimes it's better not to say anything. But sometimes what to say will come to me, and patients tell me how much they appreciate that.

What advice can you give someone thinking of becoming a nursing assistant?
Get certified. It shows you're being professional about what you do. Think positively and cater to the patient before you cater to yourself.

Tammy M. Ryan, 24,
nursing assistant, Fellowship Home, Danville, Kentucky
Years in the job: two

What do you currently do?

I work as a nursing assistant in a nursing home, from 7 A.M. until 3 P.M., five days a week. In the morning I make sure the patients are comfortable and those who have trouble controlling their bladders are dry. Then I set up trays and serve them breakfast, feeding anyone who needs to be fed. After cleaning up breakfast, I start baths. At 11:00 A.M. I take a half-hour break and then make rounds to see that everyone's comfortable. After that's done, lunch is served. If the nurses need help, I might stay overnight and help them pass out the medication, since I have a special licensed to do that.

The RNs and LPNs teach us a lot about medical things we didn't learn in training, such as how a person gets sick. I believe our elderly are important and need to be taken care of. I have the same patients every day, and I care about them and become attached to them—it's not like working in a hospital, where patients come and go.

How did you get started?

A few years ago I was laid off from my factory job and took a temporary three-month job as a nursing assistant. I enjoyed it, so I took a medical assisting course at the Danville Practical School of Nursing, then came back to the nursing home and trained.

What's the most difficult part of working in this field?

It's a lot of hard work, and you need a lot of patience. Sometimes the patients are confused and don't always know where they are. You have to take time to understand what they want. Their patience is short, and they can't understand why they have to wait for anything.

What do you like most about your work?

The appreciation I get from patients. If you get done with a bath or help feed them, they want to hug you.

What are you most proud of?
Making sure patients are taken care of. I get satisfaction out of knowing I gave a good bath or dressed them well.

What do you plan to be doing in five years?
I want to further my education in nursing. There's a two-year RN program starting in the spring, and I've thought about going into that.

What advice can you give someone thinking about going into this field?
Any person who feels that they want to be an LPN or an RN should be a nursing assistant first. Being a nursing assistant teaches you to have compassion, and you need that before you can go on.

HOME HEALTH AIDE

Home health aides are the unsung hero-
ines of the health care profession. Their
skills, patience and compassion make it possible for people who are too sick or frail to
take care of themselves to live comfortably in
the familiar surroundings of their own homes,
instead of as helpless patients in an imper-
sonal hospital or nursing home.

Home health aides care for patients with a wide
range of needs. Typically, patients are recovering from surgery or a stroke, have a chronic
disease like diabetes or Parkinson's, are elderly
or terminally ill. Some patients are well enough
to dress themselves and take a walk; others are completely
bedridden.

As a home health aide, you are a very important person
in your patients' lives. Every day you head to a patient's
house or apartment where you tend to the patient's personal

17

hygiene and grooming; change the bed; cook a light meal; help him or her move around with a walker, wheelchair or cane; and even tidy up the place. And, at least as important as the tasks above, you communicate by your attitude and conversation that you really care about your patient.

Some patients live with family members, but many elderly people live alone. You are their link to the outside world. You bring them not only the physical things they need to feel better but also your enthusiasm and hope. Since people in poor or declining health may be frustrated and depressed, they don't always show much appreciation for your efforts.

To be a home health aide you must be a "people person" with a cheerful personality and plenty of energy. You need to be able to talk easily and comfortably with people who may be different from you. You must be open minded about how other people live and like the idea of traveling to people's homes to make your rounds. You must be someone who will cherish the reward of feeling worthwhile, knowing that you help people take care of themselves and maintain their dignity, despite their illness or advanced age.

What You Need to Know

❏ Basic anatomy (the structure and organs of the human body)

❏ Basic biology (elements of body functioning, including the respiratory and urinary systems; awareness of signs of infection)

❏ Nutrition (to prepare sugar-restricted diets for diabetics or salt-restricted meals for heart patients)

❏ Hygiene (cleanliness of the surroundings and the patient to prevent and control infection)

Necessary Skills

❏ Taking vital signs (pulse, temperature, respiration and, if included in training, blood pressure)

❏ Personal hygiene (bathing, mouth care, toileting)

❏ First aid (emergency care for cuts, burns, choking, shock)

❏ CPR (cardiopulmonary resuscitation, a set of skills taught in some training programs that can revive a person who has stopped breathing or whose heart has stopped)

❏ Cooking

❏ Housekeeping

❏ The ability to engage patients in conversation and get them to talk about their physical and mental health

Do You Have What It Takes?

❏ Compassion for those who are elderly, sick and weak

❏ Excellent powers of observation (needed to watch for changes in a patient's condition)

❏ Ability to respond calmly in emergencies

❏ Concern for cleanliness and order

❏ A friendly personality

❏ Patience (those who are sick or elderly can be demanding and difficult)

❏ Kindness

Getting Into the Field

Physical Attributes

❑ Strength (this work can be hard on your back if you have to lift your patient or take him or her to the bathroom, for example)
❑ Flexibility (you do a lot of bending and stretching)
❑ Stamina (you're on your feet a lot)

Education

Before most home health care agencies will hire you, they require that you pass a test proving competence in basic mathematics and in reading and writing at the eighth-grade level. Some agencies have tougher requirements, however. For admission to its training program, for example, the Alabama Department of Public Health requires a high school diploma, GED (graduate equivalency diploma) or a tenth-grade education plus two years' experience at a nursing home or hospital.

Licenses Required

No states require a license, but many do require training that leads to a certificate.

Many home health care agencies require new employees to participate in their own agency-sponsored training program leading to a certificate even if you have already been certified elsewhere. Some agencies require that applicants take a drug screening test, a physical exam and even an FBI screen to determine that you have no criminal record. Other agencies require no testing or certification.

Job Outlook

Job openings will grow: much faster than average
Competition for jobs: very favorable opportunities

Home health aide is the fastest-growing job category in the United States between now and 2005. The government projects a 91.7 percent increase in the number of home health aides needed—from 287,000 jobs in 1990 to 550,000 in 2005.

The huge demand is due to several factors. Families

and doctors have begun to appreciate the value of caring for people in their own homes. Also, insurance companies have begun to encourage greater use of home health care because it is much less expensive to provide than hospital or nursing home care. And as the baby boomer population (people born between 1946 and 1964) ages, there will be a much greater need for medical and elder care.

Entry-level job: home health aide (sometimes called homemaker-home health aide)

As a home health aide you work for a private or state-run agency that arranges your daily schedule. You are a paraprofessional (a trained nonprofessional) health care giver who tends to patients in their own homes.

◆ **The Ground Floor**

Beginners and Experienced Home Health Aides

◆ **On-the-Job Responsibilities**

Depending on the distance you must travel to each patient and the amount of care each one requires, you usually visit four to six patients a day and perform any or all of the following tasks:

❑ Observe and record the patient's status, checking for any changes in condition and signs of infection, diarrhea, constipation
❑ Read and record vital signs (heart rate, breathing, etc.)
❑ Help the patient use the bathroom, bedside toilet or bedpan
❑ Assist a patient with personal hygiene if he or she is unable to do so (help the patient bathe, brush her teeth, comb his hair, shave)
❑ Transfer the patient to a chair or wheelchair, help her walk with a walker or cane, help him through exercises prescribed after a stroke or other illness
❑ Prepare a meal, following a dietician's orders, and help the patient eat
❑ Perform household tasks to improve hygiene of the home, such as tidying up kitchen and bathroom,

changing sheets, doing laundry, food shopping
❑ Talk with the patient's family members about his or her well-being and progress

When You'll Work

Most home health aides work a 40-hour week, from 8 A.M. to 4 P.M. or 9 A.M. to 5 P.M., Monday through Friday. But this field offers plenty of opportunity for part-time, temporary and flexible work hours, since sick people need care every day. Some aides work weekends only, others just mornings or afternoons. Almost any arrangement of hours is possible.

Time Off

Typically, full-time home health aides get two weeks' vacation and the federal holidays off.

Who's Hiring

❑ State and private home health care agencies
❑ Visiting nurse agencies

On-the-Job Hazards

❑ Exposure to infectious blood, bodily fluid or airborne viruses and diseases (it's essential to follow safety precautions)
❑ Back injuries caused by lifting

Places You'll Go

Beginners and experienced home health aides: local travel only.

If patients are well enough, you may help take them to visit family or friends or go shopping. Although most patients are too ill to travel distances, occasionally a patient may request that a home health aide accompany him or her on vacation.

Surroundings

Each patient's home means new surroundings to adapt to. Of course, some people live in beautifully maintained homes, and others live in very rundown and depressing conditions. Part of your job is to improve a patient's surroundings, if necessary, by taking steps to make them cleaner and safer.

◆ **Dollars and Cents**

Salaries start at about $5 an hour ($10,400 a year) and, with increases for merit and seniority, go up to about $18,000 a year. If you work part time, you may be paid by the visit instead of by the hour. In rural Oklahoma, for example, part-time home health aides are paid $9 per visit on weekdays, $10 per visit on weekends. You'll also be reimbursed for travel expenses, typically about 23¢ a mile.

◆ **Moving Up**

To earn a higher salary and have greater responsibility, you have to go back to school for more training. Home health aides often go on to become LPNs (licensed practical nurses) or RNs (registered nurses) or enter a related health profession.

◆ **Where the Jobs Are**

There is no shortage of jobs for home health aides anywhere in the country, and this is not expected to change. Naturally there are more jobs in more densely populated urban and suburban areas. Simply, where there are more people, there is more of a need for home health care.

◆ **Training**

High schools often provide training for home health aides at minimal cost through their adult education programs. A great number of home health care agencies and visiting nurse associations around the country offer their own training and certification programs. Some of them even pay your salary while you are being trained. Check the *Yellow Pages* under "Home Health Services" and "Nurses" for agencies to call. Also check with your county and state health departments for training and employment information from government agencies.

The typical training program consists of 75 hours of instruction, which includes 16 hours of practical training. Some programs include an additional eight hours of instruction in first aid and CPR.

The Male/Female Equation

◆ This is one field that is still almost exclusively female. Still, the field is a great way for women—or men—considering a career in nursing or other hands-on medical careers to get exposure to the world of health care with a minimum investment of time for training.

Making Your Decision: What to Consider

◆

The Bad News
❑ Low pay
❑ No career growth without more schooling
❑ Some exposure to infectious diseases
❑ Much commuting between patients' homes
❑ Little appreciation for your efforts (sometimes)

The Good News
❑ Quick training and entry to the work force
❑ Rewarding work
❑ Plenty of jobs
❑ Job security
❑ Flexible hours

WHAT IT'S REALLY LIKE

Velma Gonzales, 30,
home health aide,
Medical Home Health, Inc.,
Stillwell, Oklahoma
Years in the job: four as a home health aide,
one as a provider (a nonmedical home helper)

What do you currently do?
As a certified home health aide, I visit six people a day.
Most of the patients I see are elderly and live alone. I spend
45 minutes to an hour with each person, depending on what
they want done that day. The first thing I do is take vital
signs, then I start their personal care—cleaning, dressing
and grooming. After that I do light housekeeping, including
cooking. When a patient needs to sit and talk about problems or things on her mind, I sit there and listen.

If there are changes in a patient's condition or complica-
tions, I jot that down in my progress notes and bring them
back to the office to report to our supervisor, who is a
nurse.

Our work is countywide and covers a 50-mile radius. Right
now I'm working in two different towns. Sometimes I have

25

to travel far, but sometimes I have four or five patients in one town, within a mile of the office.

Why did you choose this field?
Caring for the elderly is something I've always done. I was raised by my grandparents, and I've always had to care for my grandma, doing her housekeeping and grocery shopping. It's a gift, being able to work with the elderly, and I love it.

How did you get started as a professional in the health field?
An elderly man I knew needed someone to take care of him. I became his "provider," staying with him for about three hours a day, doing housekeeping and taking him to the doctor or grocery store. To be a provider, a position paid for by the state, you don't need any special training—it's not a medical job.

Then a friend in nursing encouraged me to go for home health aide training. I got my nurse's aide certificate from the vocational-technical school here in town. Two weeks after that I applied to Medical Home Health for a job and was hired. They have their own home health aide training and certification program, which I took while I was working for them.

What was the hardest thing about working in this field during the first few years?
Dealing with people dying. I had to sit down and say to myself, "Well, this is your profession. This is what's going to keep happening. Can you handle it?" I don't think you ever get totally comfortable with it, but the way I handle it, as a Christian, is through prayer. Knowing there is a life after death for these people helps me a lot. But it's still hard seeing people die, people you're close to and do things for every day.

How many different jobs have you held in the medical field?
I've had just this one job as a home health aide for four years.

What do you like most about your work?
Helping make patients happy in any way I can. You love

them, and they love you back. You do things for them, and they're so pleased. You may be the only family they have—a lot of families really don't care about their elderly. It's very rewarding to know you're giving people the love and attention and care that they need.

What do you like least about your work?
The traveling you have to do to get to your patients.

What are you most proud of?
I feel I have accomplished something when I come into the office and my supervisor, after a supervisory visit, says, "These patients think you're the best." That makes my day. Sometimes you get run down and you think you're not doing any good for these people, but you are. When you hear that your patients think you're really good and they like you, that's what makes you feel good.

What do you plan to be doing in five years?
I want to go to nursing school for licensed practical nursing (LPN).

What advice would you give to someone thinking of going into home health care?
Make sure you have patience. If you don't have patience, I don't think you can do it. Working with the elderly is kind of like working with children. You have to be really careful in how you approach them—if you're in a bad mood, they know it. You can't hide things from them. You have to be able to really show them you care.

Lulu Pelletier, 38,
scheduling assistant/home health aide,
Visiting Nurses of Aroostook,
Aroostook, Maine
Years in the job: nine as a home health aide,
two as a certified nurse's aide

What do you currently do?
In the mornings I work as a scheduling assistant in the office, figuring out that day's schedule for the nurses' aides and home health aides. In the afternoons I'm a home health

aide. I've been doing this split job for about seven months. Before this promotion I was a full-time home health aide.

I work alongside four other people in a small, modern office, but it's not colorful, not "designer." About half of my scheduling work is done in this office. Some days are hectic, some are not.

Once I finish in the office, at 12:30 P.M., I spend the afternoon seeing two patients—half the usual number in a day. We're in a rural area, so I have to travel about thirty minutes each way.

Why did you choose this field?
I didn't really choose it. I was going to college for an associate degree in social work so I could work as an activities coordinator, and I had a few nights when I didn't have any classes. My best friend was in charge of adult education at the local high school, and she said, "Why don't you take the CNA (certified nurse's assistant) course to fill in the other days?" So I took the course and ended up getting a job. I never finished my degree.

Where did you first work as a CNA?
My first job was at Fort Hill Manor, a nursing home in Fort Kent, Maine. I helped clean the patients, change their clothes, feed them, take them to the bathroom or helped them use a bedpan, moved them from their bed to a chair or assisted them in their walking, made beds and did laundry. In addition, two days a week I assisted the activities coordinator. On those days I cut patients' hair (I wasn't officially trained to do that, but I had always cut my friends' hair). I organized crafts activities and family parties for them.

Was that a "usual" first job?
No. I had more responsibility than is standard for a CNA. But—I don't know how to say this without sounding immodest—I'm a take-charge person.

Did you have any preparation for this field?
For most of my life I'd taken care of a sister who was mentally retarded. And I took the CNA training course. Though taking it started out as just something to do, I found that I liked it.

What was the hardest thing about working in this field during the first few years?

At the nursing home I worked nine days in a row before I had a day off—that was a long stretch. Also, the work is very hard on your back—there's so much lifting. And you're on a schedule where you hurry all the time in order to get everyone taken care of. It's not that I mind going fast—but I feel like I'm shortchanging people. I felt bad having to interrupt them when they were talking to me so I could keep on schedule.

How did you become a home health aide?

I was hired at Visiting Nurses of Aroostook as a CNA, started working and taking their training classes at the same time. Then I took the test for state certification.

What have you learned on the job?

I learned a lot of nursing skills and personal skills—how to deal with people. I'm not as nervous as I was; I just try to do the best job I can and if a patient doesn't appreciate it one day, I think that perhaps he or she will the next day.

How many years have you spent at each of these jobs?

Two years at the nursing home and the last nine years at Visiting Nurses of Aroostook.

What do you like most about your job now?

I love the people. We all get along so well. My supervisors at Visiting Nurses allow you to grow and are open to ideas and suggestions. If you want to be creative on the job— find better ways to communicate with patients, for example—they encourage you to try.

What do you like least?

Nothing, except that I still have to watch out for my back. I left the nursing home so I would be able to continue this work without ruining my back. Now if I have to move a heavy patient, I use a hydraulic lift.

In your years on the job, what are you most proud of?

It's often hard for families when people are sick or dying. Everyone in the family is under stress. I think that having a good relationship with everybody is what I'm most proud of.

What advice would you give to someone thinking of going into this field?

I would recommend taking CNA training in high school and working in home health care for a while, maybe to put yourself through college. We have a lot of people who work part time, a lot of nursing students who work as CNAs or home health aides while they're going to school. Young people should realize that the pay is not enough to support a family, but the job would give them good experience to move on to something else in the health field.

Desiree Oakley, 27,
home health aide 1,
Morgan County Health Department,
Decatur, Alabama
Years in the job: one

What do you currently do?

Our patients range in age from infants to very aged senior citizens. Currently, my youngest patient is 22. He has cerebral palsy, and I attend to his complete personal care. All our patients are homebound. They're not able to leave the house for any reason but to go to their doctors.

I have from five to six patients at a time, some who are bedbound, others who are able to walk on their own. When I am first sent to their homes, I check to see whether they are sick or need any type of medical attention. Also, are they walking well? Are they alert, does what they say make sense, do they know who and where they are? I record their condition. I help them with their personal care. That involves a bedbath, bath or shower and all their grooming.

How much time do you spend with each patient?

It depends on the patient but usually no less than one hour. I'll do more things for bedbound patients. I'll do their laundry or dishes for them or fix them something to eat. I have some patients I spend two hours with.

How much time do you spend driving?

I'm in a rural area and our average driving time is one and a half to two hours a day. But the health department is start-

ing to "cluster" our patients so we will have a little less
driving.

Why did you choose the field of home health care?
Because I love working with people. I've had take-charge
positions before, but I had a problem: I'm too nice. I've
finally found a job where that's what I get paid for—to care
about people and be nice. I was a general manager for a
fast-food restaurant. We made over a million dollars a year.
I did a good job, but I just didn't like being pushy or bossy,
and you just have to be that way to make the business run.
Now I go home, and I get to feel good about what I've done
and never, ever dread going to work. I look forward to it.

How did you get started in home health care?
I was introduced to home health care when my grandmother
had a stroke, and my family and I cared for her at home for
two years. I had wanted to get into the medical field, but
that's how I became interested in this area.

**What kind of training did you have to become a home
health aide?**
I was hired by the Morgan County Health Department as a
home health aide based on my experience caring for my
grandmother. While I was working, I took the state certification program, which was taught part time over seven
weeks. I've been working at this job now for a year.

**How long did it take before you felt comfortable on the
job?**
When you start out, you're fearful of getting lost because
you do a lot of travel to unknown areas. My husband teased
me. He'd say, "You can't take that job—you get lost going
out of the driveway!" But I've been fine. After two or three
weeks I felt at ease.

**What has been the hardest aspect of working in this
field?**
I would like to stay with my patients and take care of them
all day. I would like to be there at night if they need me. I
want to give them my phone number and say, "Call me if
you need me and I'll be here." But you can't, you have to
draw the line. You have to say, "I'm here eight to five. I
have to go home because I have a family to take care of."
The hardest thing is knowing where to draw the line.

What do you like most about your work?
Helping people. Knowing I'm doing something good with my life, something useful. You get attached to your patients, seeing them every day. You never go through a day without hearing "thank you" or "we appreciate you."

What do you like least?
Knowing my patients' death is impending. It's hard to have to watch someone die. You wish there were some way you could rid them of all their pain. With these feelings of sadness there is also the feeling of joy to know you are there for people when they need you most.

What achievements are you most proud of?
Making a difference in a lot of people's lives. We have some patients who are so lonely; they just need somebody to talk to. I have one family that's really touched me. They live in very poor conditions. When I leave, I have to check myself to see if I have bugs on me. But they have an old rickety piano that's over in the corner, and it makes their day when I just sit down and play it for them.

What are your plans for the future?
In the fall I'm going to start school part time to become a physical therapist. Since I've been working as a home health aide, I've had a gut feeling that that's what I want to do. I plan to stay in home health—I love this program, and these people need physical therapy, which is covered by insurance and state funds. I went into home health care to see whether I'd like to be an RN, but I've found that working as an RN is kind of like social work. There's only so much you can do. But with physical therapy, you can really help them recover more.

What advice would you give to someone thinking of going into home health care?
If you're thinking of eventually being a nurse, home health care is a very good thing to do. You get good hands-on experience, and you find out if you can do this work.

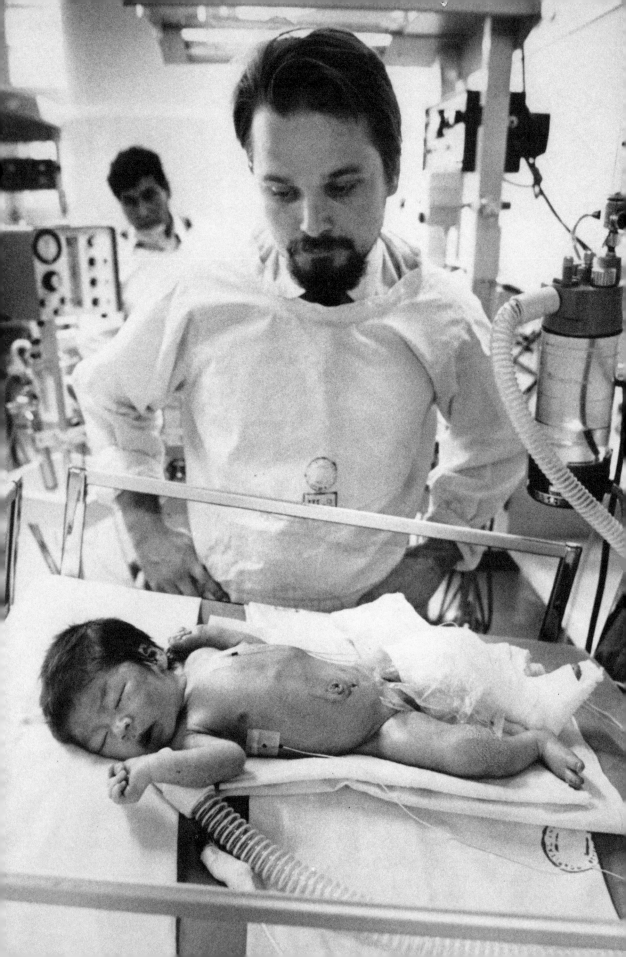

They are angels of mercy, the heartbeat of a hospital, the round-the-clock caregivers of the sick. Licensed practical nurses (LPNs) give their patients medication, regularly check their condition, give baths, make beds and, in some states, draw blood for tests. If you are compassionate, dedicated and forgiving of people who may not be capable of showing appreciation, you may do well as a modern-day Florence Nightingale.

L PNs work in hospitals, nursing homes, schools, clinics and doctors' offices. Those who work in hospitals can be found in all departments: pediatrics, maternity, general surgery and the emergency room. Those who work in specialized departments such as neonatal (newborn care) or the emergency room often receive on-the-job training to equip them with the skills necessary to be an effective member of the nursing team.

Beginners and, in most cases, experienced LPNs work under the supervision of an RN. As you learn on the job, however, you'll have more authority to give medication or draw blood or take responsibility for a patient's chart on your own.

LPNs generally don't work as nursing supervisors in big hospitals; however, they often do in nursing homes, rehabilitation hospitals, clinics or doctors' offices, where knowledge of high-tech medicine isn't as important.

You can be on the job as an LPN after just one year of training and passing a licensing exam. Because job opportunities are plentiful, you can look forward to finding a job rather easily.

Nursing is physically exhausting—you often have to be on your feet all day. And following the orders of supervising nurses and doctors can sometimes be a tall order; they may not always ask in a nice way. Still, if you are someone who would like to ease the pain of those who are suffering, you will find great satisfaction and success as an LPN.

What You Need to Know

- ❑ Biology (how the human body functions, including the respiratory, circulatory, digestive and other systems)
- ❑ Anatomy (the structure and organs of the human body)
- ❑ Pharmacology (drugs and their effectiveness against disease, their side effects and how a drug's action may change when a patient is also taking other drugs)
- ❑ Nutrition (the needs of diabetics on sugar-restricted diets and of heart patients on salt-restricted diets, for example)
- ❑ Basic medical terms and their meaning

Necessary Skills

- ❑ First aid (emergency care for cuts, burns, choking, shock)
- ❑ CPR (cardiopulmonary resuscitation—a set of skills that can revive a person who has stopped breathing or whose heart has stopped)
- ❑ Medical procedures, such as taking vital signs (temperature, blood pressure, pulse); adjusting catheters (tubes for draining urine); venipuncture (giving shots, setting up intravenous feeding and medicine tubes); phlebotomy (drawing blood for tests). Note: In most states venipuncture and phlebotomy require special licensing; some states do not allow LPNs to perform those procedures.

Do You Have What It Takes?

- ❑ Compassion for those who are sick, frightened and weak
- ❑ Excellent powers of observation (needed to watch for changes in a patient's condition)
- ❑ Ability to respond calmly under pressure in emergencies
- ❑ Concern for cleanliness and order

❏ The self-esteem to feel comfortable around and work with medical personnel who have much more education and training than you do

❏ Good health, including strong legs and back, since you'll have to support or lift patients (for instance, from a bed to a wheelchair to the bathroom)

Education

High school diploma or graduate equivalency diploma (GED), as well as the completion of a one-year program at a vocational or technical school or community college.

License Required

State license; most states will honor the licenses of other states.

**Job
Outlook**

Job openings: will grow much faster than average

Competition for jobs: plenty of openings

Licensed practical nursing is one of the fastest-growing of all occupations. Most new jobs for LPNs are expected to be in nursing homes because as baby boomers (born from 1946 to 1964) age, the number of older people and disabled needing long-term care is expected to rise rapidly. Group homes for the elderly and for the mentally disabled will also see an increased need for LPNs. And the trend toward early release of patients from hospitals will create an increasing demand for LPNs at long-term care facilities, where patients can continue to recover before returning home.

Hospital demand for LPNs, however, is not expected to grow because hospital care will continue to emphasize the intensive, high-technology treatment handled by more highly trained personnel. Hospitals could need more LPNs, however, if they continue to face an RN shortage.

Entry-level job: licensed practical nurse (LPN). (In California and Texas the title is Licensed Vocational Nurse, or LVN.)

◆ **The Ground Floor**

Beginners

◆ **On-the-Job Responsibilities**

- ❑ Give medication
- ❑ Take vital signs (temperature and blood pressure)
- ❑ Check patients' equipment, such as heart monitors and catheters
- ❑ Change bandages
- ❑ Observe patients' condition
- ❑ Keep patient charts
- ❑ Give baths
- ❑ Make beds

Experienced LPNs

Same as beginners, but if licensed for venipuncture and phlebotomy, they will also give shots, set up intravenous tubes and draw blood for tests. They may supervise other LPNs.

The typical work week is 40 hours. At hospitals and other health care facilities that operate 24 hours a day, you will have to work rotating eight-hour shifts (7 A.M. to 3 P.M., 3 P.M. to 11 P.M., 11 P.M. to 7 A.M., for example), including weekends and holidays. LPNs who work at a health maintenance organization (HMO), clinic, school or doctor's office usually work only daytime hours. If, however, the doctor's office or clinic you work for is open in the early evening or on weekends (often the case with pediatricians' offices), you may have to work those same hours. If you work overtime, you will probably get paid time and a half, and for holidays, double-time pay.

◆ **When You'll Work**

Some LPNs work part time. Others who prefer more flexibility in their hours work for temporary agencies. The pay of these per diem (paid by the day) LPNs can be high, but they may or may not receive such benefits as health insurance or vacation pay.

Time Off

After one year on the job, you will get one week of vacation; after two or three years, you will get two weeks off per year. When you can take time off often depends on seniority (how long you have been on staff).

Perks

The biggest employers offer the best perks, such as:
- ❏ Time off and paid expenses to attend seminars or meetings
- ❏ Tuition reimbursement for LPNs who want to become RNs
- ❏ Sign-on bonus (hospitals or agencies with a nursing shortage crisis)

Who's Hiring

- ❏ Hospitals (they employ about 50 percent of all LPNs)
- ❏ Nursing homes (they employ 20 percent of all LPNs)
- ❏ HMOs (health maintenance organizations, which are mini-medical centers where patients can see all kinds of medical specialists for a lower fee than is paid by a patient who has traditional health insurance)
- ❏ Clinics (private or state agencies that provide their own staff doctors for your care). Clinics usually specialize in a particular type of health care, such as OB/GYN (obstetrical/gynecological, associated with childbirth and the medical and reproductive care of women) or pediatrics (the medical care of children)
- ❏ Long-term care and rehabilitation facilities (these include nursing homes for the elderly, burn centers and rehabilitation hospitals that specialize in therapy for people recovering from accidents and strokes)
- ❏ Doctors' offices
- ❏ Hospices (where the dying are cared for in a nursing home-type setting or in their own homes)
- ❏ Temporary help agencies (these specialize in placing health care personnel)
- ❏ Schools (including grade school, high school and college health centers)

❑ Slips, trips and falls (caused by water on the floor or accidents by patients who have trouble controlling their bladders)

❑ Exposure to infectious blood, bodily fluid or airborne viruses and diseases (it's essential to follow safety precautions)

❑ Back injuries caused by lifting

LPNs are not required to be immunized against hepatitis, but it is a good idea.

◆ **On-the-Job Hazards**

Beginners and experienced LPNs: You may occasionally attend educational seminars and professional conferences around the country. Some employers pay for LPNs to attend; others give time off but don't cover expenses.

◆ **Places You'll Go**

Hospital settings vary widely in appearance: from linoleum to carpeted floors; from tastefully coordinated drapes, paint and furniture to drab, low-cost interiors; from a constant hustle-bustle to general peacefulness interrupted by the occasional emergency. Profitable private hospitals and institutions invest the most in making their facilities attractive and welcoming; budget-conscious state and city health care facilities are the least inviting.

The center of activity for LPNs is the nursing station, which is often decorated with cards and flowers for or from patients. Normally, the only view of the outdoors you'll have is the one from patients' rooms. Don't count on much privacy on the job; if you need to make a personal phone call, you will have to use a public phone in the lobby.

◆ **Surroundings**

How much you'll make depends on the type and size of the hospital or institution you work for, the region of the country it's located in and your level of experience. Large hospitals generally pay more than nursing homes; institutions in cities tend to pay more than employers in small towns or rural areas. Salaries range widely: from $13,000 in some rural areas to $30,000 in some big-city hospitals. The average salary falls somewhere in the low $20,000s.

◆ **Dollars and Cents**

Los Angeles, New York, Detroit and Washington, D.C. pay especially well; areas in the West Virginia and Ohio countryside pay poorly.

Moving Up

While an LPN's chances of upward mobility are slim in hospitals (head nurses and team leaders come from the ranks of RNs), his or her chances for promotion improve at other facilities. If you work in a doctor's office, clinic, nursing home or long-term care facility, where the focus is not on high-tech medicine, with experience you may become a nursing supervisor. You will also have more opportunity to advance if you're willing to work in rural areas where RNs are in especially short supply.

To really boost earning potential, position and responsibility, many LPNs go back to school for an RN diploma or a BS in nursing. It's the only guaranteed way to move up.

Where the Jobs Are

Nursing jobs exist wherever there are health care facilities, although there are fewer in rural areas. Jobs increase with the population. States that are heavily populated, especially by the elderly, offer many employment opportunities for LPNs. California, Florida, Texas and New York are fairly steady employers of LPNs.

Training

In all states except Texas and Washington, LPN (LVN in Texas and California) training is offered by vocational and technical schools. In Texas and Washington community colleges provide the training programs.

For a complete list of state-accredited programs, first call the National Council of State Boards of Nursing in Chicago (312-787-6555) for the phone number and address of the LPN/LVN state board in the state where you want to attend school. Then contact each individual state board for a list of schools or programs in that state. You may be charged for the list (Texas, for example, charges $5).

You can also send for a book called *State Approved Schools of Nursing LPN/LVN*, which lists all the programs in the United States and is updated annually. Specifically request Publication #19-2413 and include a check or money order for $22.95 plus $3.50 for postage and handling. Mail your request and payment to the National League for Nursing, 350 Hudson Street, New York, New York 10014, Attention: Publications.

A male nurse still raises some eyebrows—except in the Army! The U.S. Army is the only branch of the Armed Services to provide LPN/LVN training. Slowly men are discovering the rewards of nursing, and their numbers are increasing. Still, they account for only three percent of all nurses (including RNs) nationwide.

◆ **The Male/Female Equation**

The Bad News
❑ Low starting salary
❑ Low prestige (compared to the prestige enjoyed by more highly educated doctors and nurses)
❑ Night shifts and holiday work
❑ Exposure to infectious diseases

The Good News
❑ Quick training and entry to the work force
❑ Meaningful work
❑ Abundant jobs in well-populated areas
❑ Job security

◆ **Making Your Decision: What to Consider**

National Association for Practical Nursing Education & Service, Inc.
(NAPNES)
1400 Spring Street
Suite 310
Silver Spring, Maryland 20910
301-588-2491
You can write or call for a free career pamphlet and a list of nursing programs in your area, as well as details on how to purchase the NAPNES publication *The Journal of Practical Nursing*.

◆ **More Information Please**

National Federation of Licensed Practical Nursing
P.O. Box 18088
Raleigh, North Carolina 27619
919-781-4791
Call or write for a free brochure called "Profile of Practical Nursing."

National Council of State Boards of Nursing
676 N. St. Clair Street
Suite 550
Chicago, Illinois 60611-2921
312-787-6555

WHAT IT'S REALLY LIKE

Sergeant Darin D. Oberhart, 24,
licensed practical nurse/91C,
wardmaster for intermediate care ward,
41st Combat Support Hospital,
Fort Sam Houston, Texas
Years in the job: two and a half as U.S. Army
LPN, four as U.S. Army Reserves
combat medic

Why did you choose to become an LPN?
I've always been interested in the medical field. I had some
first aid training when I was 14 or 15, and one day I came
upon a serious traffic accident. I did things I didn't know I
could do. Afterward I thought, "Wow, I did that. I knew I
could have done more if I had known how." By the end of
high school, I knew I wanted to go into the medical field.

How did you become an army LPN?
I enlisted in the reserves when I was 17, with parental con-
sent because I was a minor. After basic training I went
through 91 Alpha (91A) School, a full-time, ten-week program that qualifies you as a combat medical specialist—a
combat medic. Every time I came back from the annual

45

reserves training, I'd find myself saying, "This is great. I should go on active duty." But I didn't make the big decision until I learned from recruiters that I could go to 91 Charlie (91C) School for LPN training.

What was the hardest part of working as an army LPN at the beginning?
Adapting to change. Changes occur about 1,000 times a day. If you can't adapt to change, you'll find yourself spending time being frustrated, and you won't be able to get the mission accomplished.

Do you do hands-on nursing during peacetime?
Yes. By regulation, all the medical personnel are required to spend at least one-quarter of each year in the hospital on what's called medical proficiency training (MPT). When I go on MPT, I work at BAMC (Brooke Army Medical Center at Fort Sam Houston) for three months in an ICU or emergency room. I work full time at the medical center, and I'm completely away from my unit.

During peacetime, all the professional-level personnel from our unit, RNs and above, work year round at BAMC. If we were to mobilize, these personnel would be pulled from BAMC and return to the unit.

What is a combat support hospital?
The 41st Combat Support Hospital is a 200-bed hospital in which a lot of surgery is done. We maintain four intensive care units, four intermediate care and four minimal care units. When such a hospital is put together, you have a series of connected tents with air conditioning, light and power. The equipment for each unit can be packed up and contained in a large steel box that can be transferred by train, air, ship or ground.

In what kind of surroundings was the 41st set up during the Persian Gulf War?
Barren desert. As we were traveling through Iraq, there were oases that were being irrigated for farming, but that was the only green we saw. From the hospital there were no buildings in sight.

Where did you live?
We lived in GP, or general purpose, medium tents. Those

are army canvas tents. For air conditioning we rolled up the flaps and let the air blow through!

What were your responsibilities in Saudi Arabia and Iraq during the Persian Gulf War?

I was assistant wardmaster of an ICU—intensive care unit. Every day it was part of my responsibility to make sure we had the supplies needed to provide patient care. During a mascal, or mass casualties, situation, I was one of three triage NCOs (noncommissioned officers). I would leave my post in the ICU and go to the front of the hospital; there I'd help triage (select for care according to the seriousness of their wounds) the patients as they arrived.

Was it good experience?

If a combat situation happens again, I'll be the first one to raise my hand to go and take care of the troops. But I hope it never does—I hope I never have to utilize my skills in that manner again.

Explain the role of a combat support hospital and your job in peacetime.

Our peacetime role is to ensure readiness at all times. Right now I am wardmaster for an intermediate care ward. All our equipment is currently boxed up and ready to move out; I have to make sure that it is functional, that all my vehicles, and my milvan (a five-ton military van), are ready. I also have to see that the generator assigned to my unit is functional. We perform a PMCS (preventive maintenance checks and services) on the vehicles and equipment every week.

I'm also one of the unit-training NCOs and operations NCOs. I have to make sure that the people assigned to my ward understand how all the equipment works, too, teaching them one-on-one if necessary.

What are your current work surroundings?

Most of the time I'm in an office, sometimes in the motor pool or warehouse, checking the electronic equipment in my ward.

What do you like best about your work now?

I really enjoy working with the people—not just with co-workers but also with patients. There's a lot more to nursing than just giving shots and pills. You have to be personable enough to talk to the patients, to gain their trust and help them with their fears.

What do you like the least?
It depends on the day. I'm not saying that it's always cheery, but there isn't much I don't like about my job.

Do you get any hassle about being a male nurse, since most nurses are women?
In civilian life you get some of that attitude but not in the military world. There are so many professional male nurses in the army that it's not an issue.

What are you most proud of?
Helping to save lives. When I first started in nursing, I wasn't too sure I would be able to do it. But when somebody's life depends on your doing your job no matter how gross it looks or how bad off they may be, it's a lot different.

What advice do you have for someone thinking of becoming a military nurse?
Given the cost of civilian college, it's probably one of the best options nowadays for someone coming right out of high school. A lot of people who want to get into the medical field don't realize that the military will train you and pay you while you're being trained. You learn discipline and things you could never learn anywhere else, such as how to deal with people of all backgrounds, and you're doing something really important.

Silvia Trevizo, 33,
senior LVN/LVN 3, CIGNA Healthplans, Arcadia, California
Years in the job: 13 as a bilingual LVN, three as a certified nurse's aide (CNA)

What do you currently do?
I work in the ENT (ear, nose and throat) department at CIGNA, which is an HMO, or health maintenance organi-

zation. We handle emergencies and nonemergencies. I log
patients in; take their temperature and blood pressure; auto-
clave (sterilize) instruments; assist with surgeries, including
removing skin tags, timpanoplasties (repairing damaged
ear drums), biopsies (removal of small amounts of tissue to
test for cancer) and removal of skin cancers; and repair of
tracheotomies (openings made in the neck through which a
breathing tube is inserted).

I'm certified for intravenous treatment and blood with-
drawal. And since I'm bilingual, I get paid 30¢ an hour
more than other nurses at my level.

Why did you choose this field?
Nursing was a natural choice for me, coming from a His-
panic family of seven. I was the second oldest child, and
since my older sister married very young, I was the next in
line to help support my family. I became the responsible
child, and I knew I wanted to become a nurse.

How did you get started in nursing?
In high school I took allied health classes in biology and
chemistry. Right after I graduated, I started working toward
my LVN and my associate degree at Rio Hondo Junior
College. I took the two courses required to become a certified nurse's aide (CNA), and as soon as I was certified,
while I was still going to college, I took a job as a CNA at
a local hospital. I also became certified as an emergency
medical technician, though I've never worked as one.

Was it usual for you, as an LVN, to start out as a
nurse's aide?
Yes, a lot of LVNs start out as nurse's aides. Some are
happy, though, staying as NAs.

How long did it take you to have confidence and feel
professional as an LVN?
After I graduated from school, it was another three months
before I got my license; you take your exam and then have
to wait for the results. I got a job working as a receptionist
at CIGNA while I was waiting for my license, so I became
familiar with the terminology and how CIGNA worked. I
was also still working at Queen of the Valley Hospital as a
graduate nurse after having been a nurse's aide there. I

would say that after eight months on the job as an LVN, I felt pretty confident.

How many different jobs have you held in this field?
I started at CIGNA 13 years ago, after having held one other job as a nurse's aide for about three years. But at CIGNA I've done many different things: I've worked as a surgical nurse, an orthopedic nurse and a pediatric nurse before going into ENT. At CIGNA they cross-train you so if you're placed in almost any position, you can say, "Yes, I can do it."

What do you like most about your work now?
The flexibility. I'm working part time because currently my emphasis is on my kids. I'm married and a mother of three children, ages seven, five and 19 months, and I don't want to sacrifice their early years. The flexible schedule will also allow me to go on for more training when I'm ready.

What do you like least about your work?
The AIDS epidemic. You have to be very, very cautious about being exposed to bodily fluids. We used to be rather casual about handling something that might have bodily fluids on it—perhaps just pick it up with gauze and wash our hands real quick. I worry because over the past ten years I've helped with vasectomies, breast biopsies, rectal problems, venereal warts—I wish I had been more careful. Now I'll even put on gloves to pick up a tissue from the floor.

What are you most proud of?
Being chosen this year as Nurse of the Region for the San Gabriel region of CIGNA. I was recognized for how I handled premature twins in an emergency situation. A mother brought in her two babies, about eleven months old. They came from a very poor environment. One baby had a cardiac compromise (a heart crisis); the other had a respiratory compromise (a breathing crisis). We had to stabilize them. They had to have cultures taken and blood drawn, and the one with the cardiac compromise needed an IV. I have a great deal of experience in pediatrics, so these things didn't unnerve me.

What do you plan to be doing in five years?

I'll be an RN. And I'm thinking seriously about becoming a nurse-practitioner in pediatrics (care of children) or OB/GYN (obstetrics and pregnancy) and gynecology (women's reproductive health). A nurse-practitioner takes specialized training after becoming an RN and has a lot of authority. On the OB floor I would be able to do pelvic exams and Pap smears and deal with a lot of gynecological problems. In pediatrics I could handle most situations; if I had a problem or a question, I would see the physician on the floor.

What advice would you give to someone thinking of going into this field?

Be aggressive. Take any allied health courses that high schools offer. Go to junior colleges and find out what they offer. Read about the different medical fields to determine whether you really want to pursue one. Take a short training program to become an operating room technician or an emergency medical technician, for example, so you can get into the field and try it.

Peggy Weaver, 28,
associate nurse, Bryn Mawr Rehabilitation Hospital, Bryn Mawr, Pennsylvania
Years in the job: seven as an LPN, one as a nursing assistant

What do you currently do?

I work in the brain injury unit of Bryn Mawr Rehabilitation Hospital, a 120-bed suburban facility. The patients in my unit have had a traumatic injury from an accident—in a car or boat, on a motorcycle, from a fall; or they have had a nontraumatic brain injury, from a stroke, tumor or aneurysm (a blood clot in a vein or artery). They are sent to Bryn Mawr Rehab to recover as fully as they can, so they can return to work, school or their community.

I am responsible for the total care of three or four patients during my shift, from 7 A.M. to 3 P.M. My job is to help schedule and carry out the treatment ordered by the patient's team: his or her physician, primary nurse (my supervisor), the physical therapist, occupational therapist, speech pathologist, psychologist and neurologist. I dress the patients in street clothes, help them with personal hygiene and meals, move them in and out of wheelchairs, administer medication, do "trach" care (clean and adjust the breathing tubes of patients who have had tracheotomies).

The patients are in various forms of therapy from about 8 A.M. until 4 P.M. I observe, assist and follow through with the therapist's turning and out-of-bed schedule, and with requests from the therapists for positioning casts and devices to improve the patients' muscle tone.

Why did you choose this field?
My mother is an LPN in a hospital emergency room, and my father is a sixth-grade teacher. I always knew I wanted to nurse and teach, and at Bryn Mawr Rehab I do both.

How did you get started in nursing?
One summer during high school I volunteered as an escort in the acute care unit at a local hospital. I transferred patients from their rooms for X-rays or therapy.

After high school I worked as a nursing assistant doing personal patient care at a nursing home. I was trained on the job. Working as an NA, I was able to save up money to go to nursing school. I got my LPN degree in about a year and a half and started working as an LPN in a nursing home.

Was your first job, as a nursing assistant, a "usual" first job?
Yes, it's an easy way to start in the nursing field.

How long did it take you to get established as an LPN?
After you finish nursing school, you have to take your state licensing exam and then wait a couple of months to find out whether you've passed. When you get the letter in the mail and it starts out "Congratulations," you know. You're now licensed. I began working as an LPN the very next month.

What was the hardest part of working in this field during the first few years?
When I started in the nursing home, the hardest part was

taking care of a patient for months and then watching him slowly deteriorate and die. It was my first experience with the death of someone I had nursed every day.

What do you like most about your work?
I enjoy helping people reach their fullest potential. I also like the fact that I'm always learning on the job. When I started at Bryn Mawr Rehab, I didn't know anything about brain injuries, but the nursing department and therapy departments trained me. I've been there six years and I'm still learning. You never stop learning.

What do you like least?
Not seeing some of these kids come out of their semi-comatose, or half-conscious, state. Sometimes you just wish there were a pill you could give them to make them get better. It's a constant struggle watching the family try to deal with it, too—when they see the progress another patient is making and wonder why it can't be their loved one who's getting better.

What achievements are you proudest of?
I'm very proud when I see my patients' progress, when they come back and visit and they're much better than when they left. Maybe they'll go out in a wheelchair and come back walking, then say, "See what you did for me?"

What do you plan to be doing in five years?
I expect to have my RN diploma or BSN (bachelor's of science in nursing). I really enjoy working in rehab, but I'm not sure I'll continue with it because there are going to be so many more opportunities for me as an RN. "One day at a time" is how I work with my patients and their families, and that's what I tell myself, too.

What advice do you have for someone thinking of going into this field?
Do what I did. If you're unsure of what type of health profession you want to get into, do volunteer work in health care or start out as a nursing assistant. NAs are very much needed and appreciated, and the work will give you a taste of what you'd be getting into. And while you're working, you can start to save money for the next step in your education.

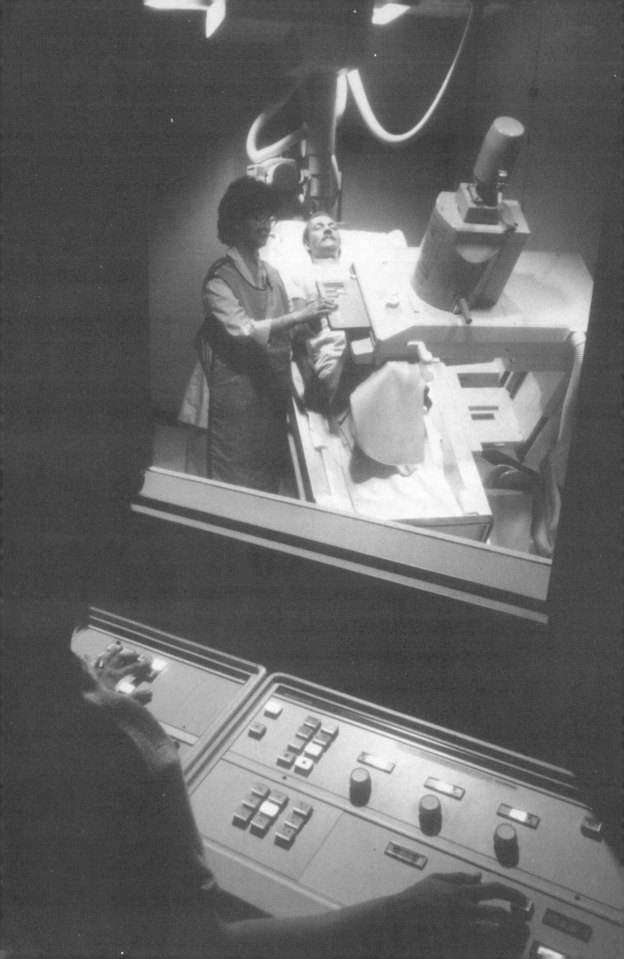

Radiologic technologists are involved in almost every type of medical problem, from a simple broken finger to life-threatening heart surgery. They are X-ray and computer imaging systems experts who take diagnostic pictures. The pace is fast, but the procedures must be done very carefully, since the pictures are critical to determining the right treatment for the patient.

Radiologic technologists do not try to explain the X-rays or pinpoint a patient's medical problem; it is against their code of ethics to do so. Making a diagnosis is the job of the radiologist, a physician.

Even on their first day on the job, radiologic technologists are expected to know exactly how to operate the whole range of radiographic equipment used for diagnosis. In a

55

small hospital you may rotate through many departments, from neonatology (newborn care) to emergency to the intensive care unit—all in one day. At a large hospital you will probably rotate among the various departments over the course of weeks or months.

Although the majority of radiologic technologists work in hospitals, they can also be found in clinics, public health care facilities and doctors' offices. Some specialize in particular types of procedures. If you work at a mammography clinic, for example, you may perform several different procedures in a day, but they will all have to do with breast care.

In addition to operating X-ray machines, radiologic technologists also operate fluoroscopes (instruments that light up the path taken by a dye, called "contrast material," swallowed by or injected into the patient). Fluoroscopy actually shows a moving picture of a body part. The patient drinks a contrast material, usually barium, that allows X-rays to project an image on a fluorescent screen. Fluoroscopy is used for examining the stomach or colon and in surgery when removing the gall bladder, performing hip replacement and inserting pacemakers.

Radiologic technologists who do the work described above are often called radiographers. There are other job specialties within the field of radiologic technology.

If you go on for additional education (beyond the required minimum two years of study), you can become a radiation therapy technologist and learn how to use radiation in cancer treatment. Or you can become a nuclear medicine technologist and use radiopharmaceuticals to diagnose or treat patients. You can specialize in mammography (breast X-ray), in sonography (which uses sound waves to take pictures) or magnetic resonance imaging (MRI), which uses magnetic waves. You can become a cardiovascular interventional technologist specializing in heart X-rays or a computer tomographer (CT or CAT-scan specialist), using computer-operated X-ray equipment.

Radiologic technologists have a talent for math and a way with people; they must operate complicated, computerized machinery with precision while also making patients feel comfortable and at ease. If that description fits you, there's no better way to be involved in the world of medicine than in the field of radiologic technology.

What You Need to Know

❑ Anatomy (the organs, bones and systems of the human body and how each works)

❑ Basic computer operation

❑ Medical terminology (so you can converse with the medical team)

❑ Radiation physics and principles of radiography (how radiation is produced and how it is used in making photographic images)

❑ Radiologic film processing

❑ Radiation protection (safety precautions required to prevent overexposure to radiation)

Necessary Skills

❑ First aid (for emergencies)

❑ Cardiopulmonary resuscitation (CPR—a set of skills that can revive a person who has stopped breathing or whose heart has stopped)

❑ Taking vital signs (pulse rate, body temperature, breathing rate, blood pressure)

❑ Venipuncture (giving injections)

❑ Ability to give clear directions in a calm, soothing way and earn the cooperation of patients who are sick, injured or frightened

Do You Have What It Takes?

❑ The "stomach" for blood

❑ Compassion for patients

❑ Strong interest in high-tech equipment

❑ The ability to be organized and detail oriented

❑ Capacity to stay calm in emergencies

❑ The self-confidence to deal with doctors

❑ Team spirit (you will have to work closely with emergency medical technicians, nurses, doctors and hospital support staff)

Physical Attributes

❑ Manual dexterity (required for positioning patients and setting the machinery precisely)
❑ Strength (you're often required to lift patients from a wheelchair to the radiologic equipment, carry several "cassettes" of X-ray film at a time and work with your hands above your head, positioning equipment)
❑ Stamina (you're on your feet almost all day)

Education

AS (associate of science) or AAS (associate of applied science) degree in radiography or a two-year hospital-based program leading to a certificate in radiography.

Licenses Required

Most states that do not have their own licensing exam (about half of them do not) require that you take and pass the national registry exam administered by the American Registry of Radiologic Technologists. Only graduates of programs approved by the American Medical Association's Committee on Allied Health Education and Accreditation (CAHEA) are eligible to do so. Even if you live in a state that has its own licensing exam, it's advisable to take the national registry exam as well; if you ever move out of the state, your national registry will probably allow you to work in the new state; your original state license alone will not.

Job Outlook

Job openings will grow: much faster than average
The Bureau of Labor Statistics projects that job openings will increase by 70 percent across the country between 1990 and 2005. The reason: The growth and aging of the population and the greater role that radiologic technologies are playing in the diagnosis and treatment of disease. Job prospects for graduates of accredited programs are excellent.

Entry-level job: radiologic technologist

The Ground Floor

Beginners and experienced radiologic technologists (who work in hospitals) may do some or all of the following:

On-the-Job Responsi-bilities

❏ Transfer patients from a wheelchair or gurney (a wheeled cot or stretcher) to the X-ray machine and position their body precisely for picture taking
❏ Take vital signs
❏ Document patient history, tests performed and other necessary data
❏ Take safety precautions for the patient and yourself to prevent unnecessary exposure to radiation
❏ Use general radiography equipment for X-rays of head, chest, back, arms and legs, hands and feet
❏ Operate fluoroscopy equipment (or assist the physician, a radiologist)
❏ Use portable equipment in the ICU (intensive care unit), surgery and neonatology
❏ Work in trauma (emergency) care
❏ Inject patients with contrast material for certain procedures, such as a kidney exam
❏ Perform mammography
❏ Process the X-ray film
❏ Evaluate the quality of the processed film to see if a diagnosis can be made from the picture taken
❏ Interact with radiologists, attending physicians, nurses and hospital support staff

Most radiologic technologists work a 40-hour week, but that may be on rotation, as nurses work (e.g., 7 A.M. to 3 P.M., 3 P.M. to 11 P.M., 11 P.M. to 7 A.M.). Some larger hospitals give you a choice of permanent shift hours, but many smaller hospitals don't have a big enough staff to cover three shifts, so you have to rotate or at least be on call at times. You probably will have to work weekends and holidays, at least occasionally. You are paid extra for

When You'll Work

overtime, holiday and on-call work. Part-time and temporary work is also common in this field.

Time Off

Typically, full-time radiologic technologists get two weeks of vacation for the first one to five years on the job. You may get three weeks off after as little as three years on the job, but more often after five years. You'll likely get four weeks of vacation after five to eight years. You may have to work some federal holidays.

Perks

❑ Paid time off while you attend seminars
❑ Tuition coverage for study in a specialty of radiologic technology

Who's Hiring

❑ Hospitals
❑ HMOs (health maintenance organizations), which are mini-medical centers where patients can see all kinds of medical specialists for a lower fee than is paid by a patient who has traditional health insurance
❑ Clinics (private or state agencies that provide their own staff doctors for your care). Clinics usually specialize in a particular type of health care, for example, OB/GYN (obstetrical/gynecological, associated with childbirth and the medical and reproductive care of women)
❑ Public health care clinics
❑ Diagnostic imaging centers
❑ Urgent care clinics
❑ Cancer hospitals
❑ Private doctors' offices

On-the-Job Hazards

❑ Small risk of exposure to radiation
❑ Exposure to infectious blood, bodily fluids or airborne viruses and diseases (it's essential to follow safety precautions)
❑ Risk of back injuries caused by lifting

Beginners and experienced radiographers: good potential for travel.

If you are interested in sampling what life is like in different places around the country (and building your savings), you can work for an agency that will place you in a temporary job. Called *locum tenens* (Latin for local temporaries), these agencies place technologists at hospitals and other institutions that are short staffed. Usually you have to commit to work at a particular location for at least four to six weeks. You're paid an hourly rate, and—the big bonus—your travel expenses, room, board and insurance are paid for. You can earn a much higher hourly rate as a locum tenens technologist than as a permanent hospital staff member. Most locum tenens agencies have been set up by entrepreneurs who are radiologic technologists or nuclear medicine technologists themselves. Such jobs are advertised in professional journals.

If you work in a hospital, chances are the radiology department is in the basement, so you may see daylight only on your lunch break. The radiology departments of some older hospitals have stark, bare walls, while newer facilities tend to have warmer environments, with murals and soothing colors on the walls. In a modern mammography clinic or imaging center, you often find attractive artwork, carpeting and color-coordinated furniture.

Salaries for radiologic technologists range from about $18,000 to about $34,000. That wide range includes beginners in lower-paying rural areas as well as highly experienced people in higher-paying metropolitan regions. Radiation therapy technologists and nuclear medicine technologists earn the highest salaries. Locum tenens earn as much as $20 to $30 an hour.

Many hospitals offer experienced technologists who want to specialize the opportunity to learn more through a formal certification program (such as those for radiation

Places You'll Go

Surroundings

Dollars and Cents

Moving Up

therapy and nuclear medicine technologists) or in a noncertification in-hospital program (such as those for mammography, diagnostic medical sonography, cardiovascular interventional technology, CT scan and MRI). You may also have the opportunity to increase your responsibility and salary by becoming an educator at your own institution.

Some technologists use their background to switch into sales. They become "technical applications specialists," sales representatives for the manufacturers of radiography equipment. They train the staff of an institution purchasing the new equipment in how to use it properly. Although this job change usually brings an increase in salary, it also means a move out of hands-on medicine.

Where the Jobs Are

There are openings for radiologic technologists all over the country in every type of facility that employs them. Generally there are more job openings in urban and suburban centers than in rural areas simply because a larger population creates a larger demand for health care.

The Male/Female Equation

According to the American Society of Radiologic Technologists, the field is 74 percent female and 26 percent male. As salaries have increased over the past five years, radiologic technology has been attracting more men.

Making Your Decision: What to Consider

The Bad News
❑ Stress due to the fast pace, unpredictability of the day's schedule and often urgent nature of the job
❑ Physically demanding work
❑ Small risk of exposure to radiation
❑ Having to work a rotating shift

The Good News
❑ Challenging, meaningful work
❑ Plenty of jobs
❑ Job security
❑ Recognition as a vital part of the medical team

Choosing a program that meets the academic requirements of the American Medical Association's Committee on Allied Health Education and Accreditation (CAHEA) is important: It's the only way you are eligible to take the national registry exam. Many employers won't hire you unless you've passed it.

The majority of programs are hospital based and lead to a certificate (many charge tuition of just several hundred dollars). There are also a large number of associate degree programs at community colleges. (Just a few vocational-technical schools offer CAHEA-approved programs.)

To get into such a program, you need a high school diploma or GED (graduate equivalency diploma), and you need to have good grades in general, but especially in math, science and English. To meet some program entry requirements you may need to go back and take a math or science course in the adult education division of a high school or the continuing education department of a college before you can be admitted. You may also need to take the SAT (Scholastic Aptitude Test), an examination used by a number of four-year colleges to determine your competency in English, math and science.

A radiologic technologist's education combines extensive classroom study and hospital-based experience. Throughout the two-year program you are tested in academic subjects as well as on your ability to communicate with patients, to position patients properly for procedures and to operate the whole range of equipment you will be expected to handle.

Currently there are separate CAHEA-approved education programs for the jobs of radiographer, radiation therapy technologist and nuclear medicine technologist. Diagnostic medical sonographer is the next specialty for which a separate educational program will be required. According to the American Society of Radiologic Technologists (ASRT), over the next few years the jobs of mammographer and cardiovascular interventional technologist, followed by computer tomographer (CAT-scan specialist) and magnetic resonance imaging (MRI) technologist, may

School Information

all require specialized formal education. Right now, however, people holding these last five jobs are trained as radiologic technologists and get specialized education on the job or in programs arranged by their hospital or other employer.

For a list of CAHEA-approved programs in radiography, radiation therapy technology, nuclear medicine technology and diagnostic medical sonography, write or call the American Society of Radiologic Technologists.

Professional Organizations

American Society of Radiologic Technologists (ASRT)
15000 Central Avenue, S.E.
Albuquerque, New Mexico 87123-3909
505-298-4500

The ASRT represents all technologists within the radiologic sciences and speaks for the profession. They publish the professional journal *Radiologic Technology* and can answer questions about education and careers in the field.

American Registry of Radiologic Technologists
1255 Northland Drive
Mendota Heights, Minnesota 55120
612-687-0048

The ARRT is the national certifying organization for radiologic technologists. Write or call for information about the certification requirements and exam so you can determine if the program you are enrolling in will adequately prepare you for it.

Society of Diagnostic Medical Sonographers
12770 Coit Road, Suite 508
Dallas, Texas 75251
214-239-7367

The field of diagnostic medical sonography is changing rapidly, and the society keeps its members informed about new technology, research and on-the-job issues in the *Journal of Diagnostic Medical Sonography*. To receive their pamphlet ''Career Information,'' send a self-addressed, stamped, business-size envelope to the address above.

American Registry of Diagnostic Medical Sonographers
2368 Victory Parkway, Suite 510
Cincinnati, Ohio 45206
513-281-7111

This is the national certifying organization for the field. Write or call for information about the certification requirements and exam so you can determine if the program you are enrolling in will adequately prepare you for it.

Society of Nuclear Medicine, Technologist Section
136 Madison Avenue
New York, New York 10016
212-889-0717

This is the professional organization for physicians as well as technologists in nuclear medicine. You can write for literature about careers in the field. They publish the *Journal of Nuclear Medicine Technology* for their technologist members.

Nuclear Medicine Technology Certification Board
2970 Clairmont Road, Suite 610
Atlanta, Georgia 30329-1634
404-315-1739

Write or call for information about the certification requirements and exam so you can determine if the program you are enrolling in will adequately prepare you for it. The ARRT (listed above) also provides such information for this specialty.

Linda Sylvia, 33,
radiologic technologist (mammographer),
Women's Diagnostic Medical Group,
Beverly Hills, California
Years in the job: 11

How did you break into this field?
I got my associate in science degree in radiologic technology at the Community College of Rhode Island in Lincoln.
I actually started working at my first job before I graduated
because there's such a demand for technologists.

Describe your first job and what you did on it.
I worked full time as a radiologic technologist in a 150-bed
hospital in the town where I lived. I did general diagnostics,
surgery and trauma. I stayed there about a year and a half,
then I quit and took a three-month vacation. My education
program was 24 months long, with just one week off at
Christmas and one in the summer. Since I started working
before I even finished school, I really needed a vacation.

When I returned, I went to work at a doctors' office, a
small private practice. But I didn't like that at all; it felt
claustrophobic after the hospital—it wasn't busy enough.

So when a position opened up at the hospital where I had originally worked, I went back there full time. I also started working part time at the hospital I had trained at.

You worked full-time and part-time jobs simultaneously?

A lot of technologists do that because it's not a real high-paying job. It pays a lot less than nursing (RN), although within the past few years the pay has increased because there's such a demand for technologists.

What kind of school preparation or background did you have for this field?

As a child with a back problem, I had X-rays on a regular basis. I was intrigued by what you could see. I knew I always wanted to go into the health field, and I was a candy-striper in high school. I decided to go into X-ray work rather than nursing because I knew I liked looking at the pictures.

What was the hardest part of working in this field at the beginning?

Working hands on with physicians, especially surgeons, who are a moody group of people. It's like a big test when you're starting out. They try to see how far they can push you. But you can't let them intimidate you; you have to stand your ground and let them know that you know what you're doing. Once they're confident of that, they tend to leave you alone. But when you go to a new job, it's the same old thing: You have to prove yourself again.

How long did it take to earn a decent salary?

It took about six years.

How many jobs have you held over your 11 years in this field?

This is my sixth job.

What do you currently do?

I work at a breast care center as one of three full-time technologists. We do mammography, or breast X-rays, to look for cancer. We also do special procedures on breasts.

All these procedures use X-ray, so we take the pictures. A lot of the procedures are sterile, so we assist by handing the doctor the instruments and keeping everything sterile.

We also stay there with the patient when the doctor leaves, never leaving the patient alone. This is a high-anxiety experience for women, and a lot of them pass out, so we're there to keep them calm and talking.

What do you like most about your work?
It's very fast paced. You're always learning because it's constantly changing. It keeps your brain active. Also, I work with a terrific group of people—the best I've ever worked with.

What has given you the most satisfaction?
Doing this job. It's such a diverse combination of things. I work on quality assurance (following up on patients to make sure they have a biopsy or other procedure that is recommended). Also, the doctor I work for has written a couple of articles for journals, and I compiled all the data for him, which was interesting and fun. I learned a lot by doing that.

What do you see yourself doing in five years?
I'd like to have kids. I probably would still work part time just to keep up with what's going on, since this field changes constantly. You can work on your own and freelance or work as a fill-in technologist at a medical facility.

What advice can you give someone thinking of going into this field?
It requires a lot of hard work and studying. You have to be real good in math and physics. You have to have a strong stomach when it comes to working in the hospital. If you're the type of person who likes to be challenged, I think this is a good field for you.

Nathan Elliott, 26,
radiologic technologist,
St. John's Lutheran Hospital,
Libby, Montana
Years in the job: four

How did you break into this field?

I went to a two-year, hospital-based program in radiography. I chose the field because I knew I could take a course where I didn't have to spend four or more years studying. I could get it done in two years and get a good job. And I had a really good deal. My program (at Columbus Hospital in Great Falls, Montana) cost only $200, including books. I just had to pay for room and board.

I was offered a job in the city where I went to school, and I loved most of the people I had been working with there, but I didn't like the doctor I had to work with. Also, I was partial to moving back to my home town.

Describe your job and what you do.

St. John's Lutheran Hospital is really small—it's got 28 beds, and it's the only hospital in the town of Libby. Because it's so small, I do a lot of things besides the usual work of a radiographer. The hospital recently got a new CT (computer tomography) scanner, so I've learned how to do CT. The hospital also ended up buying a brand-new Toshiba ultrasound machine, so I'm in the process of taking a correspondence course in ultrasound. I'm what's called registry-eligible. I have enough hours doing ultrasound to become registered if I pass the registry exam.

In the morning we usually schedule fluoroscopy. That includes upper GIs (gastrointestinal tract—the small intestine) and lower GIs (large intestine) and also IVPs (intravenous pylograms), which are pictures of the kidneys, ureter and bladder. For the upper and lower GIs you have to prepare the patient's system with a barium enema. That cleans out their bowels and inserts barium, a contrast material, into the intestine so any abnormality shows up on the fluoroscopy screen. IVP uses a different type of contrast material that you inject right into a blood vessel or organ.

These procedures are planned ahead of time, and they take a little while, so we schedule them for the morning. But on top of that, you have people coming in and out for chest X-rays and for emergencies. If you have a car accident, you have to work around everything else. In the afternoon we usually have a couple of CTs or an ultrasound. We have an orthopedic doctor in town who works in the hospital-owned clinic across the street, so we'll go across the street and take X-rays there. There's also a prompt care clinic, which is like an urgent care clinic—for things that need attention but aren't serious emergencies, like twisted ankles, hurt arms, even colds, and we take X-rays there.

What kind of preparation or background did you have for this field from school or from other experiences?
My mom's a nurse. Also, when I was taking college courses I met a girl who was thinking of going into X-ray, and she knew a little bit about it.

How long did it take before you felt you were earning a decent salary?
When you go from making nothing as a student to making $8 or $9 an hour, you feel like you're rich! At the beginning of the second year, I felt that for the size of my hospital and the area I'm in, I was doing okay.

What do you like most about your work?
I like working with the people—not just the people I work with, but also with the patients. You talk to them, get to know them a little bit. That's fun. I also like it when you feel like you're really helping somebody. Sometimes you feel like you're doing the same old thing, but there are times when you really feel like you make a difference.

What do you like least?
The hardest thing for me is being on call so much. There are three full-time technologists, including my boss. We work until 5 P.M. and then we take turns being on call all night long and on weekends. When it's your weekend, you work for four hours on Saturday, but you're also on call the rest of the entire weekend.

What has given you the greatest sense of pride in your career?
Just being in a field where you can care for people. Some-

times it's hard to keep a caring attitude, and it can get depressing because there are days you think you're not really helping anybody. But when someone who's been in a car accident comes in and you know what you're supposed to do—how to get the X-ray without having to move the patient in case the neck is broken—just being able to do that makes you feel good.

What do you see yourself doing in five years?
I'd like to be registered in ultrasound. I'm also thinking about getting my BA in business administration because I'd like to get into management of a radiology department some time down the road.

What advice would you give to someone thinking of going into this field?
Work your tail off as a student. I see students complain and complain about how hard they're working, but they've got to realize they're only in school for two years. Do the job and get it done. The people that you work with while you're a student know if you're a hard worker or not. If you are, you'll get a real good recommendation from them, and you can pretty much get a job wherever you want.

Lori Johnson, 24,
special procedures technologist,
Abbott Northwestern Hospital,
Minneapolis, Minnesota
Years in the job: four

How did you first become interested in the field?
When I was a junior in high school, I wrote a paper on the job I'd be most interested in for a health occupations class. I knew an X-ray technologist so I chose the field of X-ray for my paper. I did a lot of research on the duties of the job and the salaries, and that really piqued my interest.

How did you break into the field?
When I finished high school, I knew I didn't want to go to a four-year college. At that time a nearby hospital was offering a tuition-free X-ray training program; you only had to pay for books and a couple of courses at an affiliated

university. I thought, "I'll give this a shot." I wouldn't be out much money if I didn't care for the work, and if I wanted to go on with school, I'd have my training behind me and be able to support myself.

Describe your first job.
I had two months left until graduation when I got hired as a part-time X-ray technologist by the hospital where I was training. Once I graduated, I was hired full time, and after I passed my registry exam, I got the title "registered radiologic technologist." I did general diagnostic X-rays, I rotated into the OR (operating room), I did fluoroscopy—all the things a radiographer is trained to do.

Was it a "usual" first job?
Yes. A lot of people who train at a hospital-based program will stay on at that hospital after graduation because they know the radiologists, they know the routines and the equipment, and they feel comfortable there.

What was the hardest part of working in this field at the beginning?
Getting used to the responsibility. When you're a student, you always have your teaching technologist to rely on. When you're a technologist yourself, it's just you, the machine, the patient and the doctor. You're the one who takes responsibility for those films, and you can't blame someone else.

How long did it take you to get established and feel comfortable?
I felt really comfortable and confident by the end of the first year on the job. It takes a while in a trauma situation because the decisions have to be made so quickly and the patient could be dying. You're in there having to take pictures surrounded by surgeons and anesthesiologists and a lot of people. You have to be able to take control of the situation and feel comfortable with your work.

How many different jobs have you held in this field?
Two. I now work at Abbott Northwestern Hospital in downtown Minneapolis. It's a big hospital with more than 800 beds. I work primarily in the OR. I'm called a special procedures technologist. In OR there's a lot of variety—orthopedic (bone) surgery, back surgery, fluoroscopy. More

and more they're using X-ray in the operating room.

What do you like most about your job?

Working with people. You have to be a people person to work in any kind of job in the health field. People appreciate it when you treat them in a very professional and friendly manner. If you can talk and smile, it makes them feel more at ease.

I also like the challenge. The physicians are waiting for your picture, and if it's not precise, you have to repeat it. The danger with that is having to expose the patient to radiation again and keep him or her under anesthesia longer in order to take the picture again.

What's the hardest part of your job?

Lots of times you have a real difficult case, and that's a challenge. Say a person comes in with a major fracture of an arm or a leg. It's not the routine you learned in school—she can't move on her side or turn the way she's supposed to for the best picture, so you have to think of different angles to use and figure out how to get the picture. There's a lot of mind work involved.

What are you most proud of so far?

When I was a student, I received the Outstanding Student Award. It's not academic, it's more clinical—for how you handle your patients and do your job.

What do you plan to be doing in five years?

I'm going to continue my education here in the hospital-based program for ultrasound so I can become a diagnostic medical sonographer.

Then, in five years, I expect to be working as a diagnostic medical sonographer in a clinic where you don't have to work rotations or weekends. I'd like to be able to have a family and work nine to five with weekends off.

What advice can you give someone thinking of going into this field?

If you're still in high school, take as much math and science as you can—biology, anatomy and physics. You have to have good communication skills; a lot of the patients can be difficult to deal with. They're weak or in pain. You have to let them tell you how they can help you. You have to have patience.

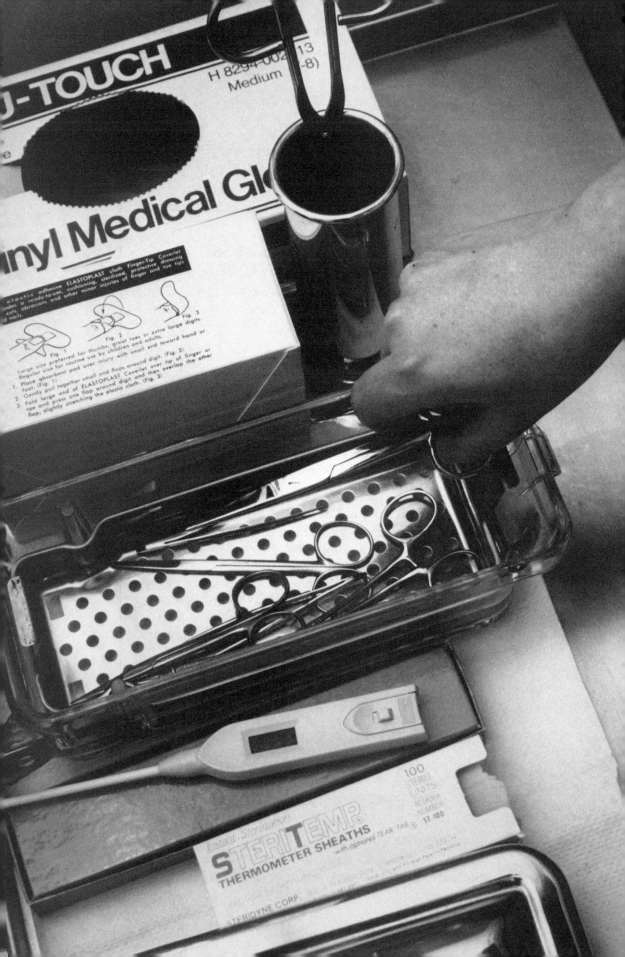

They're the backbone of doctors' offices, they greet and talk to patients and keep the doctors organized and prepared to examine patients. Being a medical assistant is the perfect job for people who love action; there is rarely an unoccupied moment during the day. You will work directly with patients and act as the "front person," explaining procedures, reassuring the ill-at-ease and providing feedback to both doctor and patients.

Medical assistants have patients fill out medical histories, pull their charts and usher them into the examining room. They give patients instructions about undressing, using a hospital gown and positioning themselves on the examining table. If they are handling clinical tasks, they will weigh patients, get a urine sample, take their blood pressure and perform other simple medical procedures. They may also assist the doctor during the examination and hand him or her instruments or prepare cultures for the laboratory. Ophthalmic medical assistants help ophthalmologists care for their patients' eyes.

Medical assistants work mostly in outpatient settings such as private doctor's offices, group practices and clinics. Some assistants concentrate on the "front office"—the administrative aspects of the job, such as insurance billing, scheduling appointments and answering phones. Others focus on the "back office"—the clinical aspects of medical assisting, such as taking vital signs or weighing and measuring patients. The larger the size of the practice where you work, the more likely it is that you can concentrate on one or the other function. Medical assistants who work in hospitals generally focus on admissions, the medical records office or the emergency room.

As a medical assistant, you have the benefit of learning from nurses and doctors by watching what they do and helping them examine and treat patients. If you want to work in the health care field but prefer hours that are regular, and you like an office environment rather than the hubbub of a hospital ward, you may find that being a medical assistant is your niche.

What You Need to Know

- ❑ Basic anatomy (the structure and organs of the human body)
- ❑ Basic physiology (the way major body systems, such as circulatory and respiratory, work)
- ❑ Medical terms (so that you can talk easily with the doctor and other health care professionals)
- ❑ Medical law and accepted rules of professional conduct
- ❑ Basic math
- ❑ Office safety procedures (in case of fire, earthquake, etc.)

Necessary Skills

- ❑ Ability to clearly communicate instructions and information to patients
- ❑ CPR (cardiopulmonary resuscitation, a set of skills that can help revive a patient whose heart has stopped or who has stopped breathing)
- ❑ First aid (for treating minor wounds, burns, etc.)
- ❑ Computer basics (word processing, for instance)
- ❑ Billing procedures

Do You Have What It Takes?

- ❑ Patience to deal with confused or difficult patients
- ❑ Friendly personality
- ❑ Respect for a patient's privacy and an ability to keep information about him or her confidential

Physical Attributes

- ❑ Strong back and legs (you may be on your feet much of the time if you're doing clinical work)
- ❑ Well-groomed appearance and good hygiene
- ❑ Manual dexterity (nimble fingers, which are necessary for tasks that require precise movements)
- ❑ Good vision (to accurately read small-print measurements on tubes, needles and other instruments)

Education

High school diploma encouraged but not required. A one- or two-year program in medical assisting is recommended.

Licenses Required

No license is required, but a growing number of medical assistants are getting certified or registered by the major professional groups, the American Association of Medical Assistants (AAMA), American Medical Technologists (AMT) and the Joint Commission on Allied Health Personnel in Ophthamology.

Job Outlook

Job openings will grow: much faster than average

The job of medical assistant is expected to be one of the fastest growing of all the occupations the federal government tracks. The number of medical assistant positions is projected to increase from 165,000 in 1992 to 287,000 in 2005, a startling rise of 73.9 percent.

The Ground Floor

Entry-level job: medical assistant

Medical assistants who work in small offices or clinics must often handle both administrative and clinical tasks. You can, however, specialize in one or the other if you plan to work for a group practice.

On-the-Job Responsibilities

While beginning and experienced medical assistants do essentially the same job, experience allows assistants interested in administrative work to assume more responsibility in office management and those interested in clinical work to do more complicated procedures, such as blood or lab work or diagnostic tests.

Beginners (administrative tasks)

❑ Handle simple insurance claims billing
❑ Schedule and greet patients, ask first-time patients to

fill out medical history
- ❏ Prepare and maintain medical records
- ❏ Perform secretarial tasks and transcription (take clear medical notes from dictation or written records)
- ❏ Send out bills and reminders to patients
- ❏ Answer phones and handle correspondence
- ❏ Act as the doctor's representative—passing along and, when necessary, simplifying information between the physician and patients

Experienced Medical Assistants (administrative tasks)

- ❏ Handle complicated insurance coding and billing
- ❏ Supervise the work of less experienced medical assistants
- ❏ Negotiate contracts for office and medical equipment leases and supplies
- ❏ Track and balance office income and expenditures

Beginners (clinical tasks)

- ❏ Take vital signs (pulse rate, breathing rate, blood pressure)
- ❏ Record patient medical histories
- ❏ Prepare patients for procedures (give instructions on undressing, wearing a hospital gown and positioning the body on the examining table)
- ❏ Collect and do simple lab tests on specimens (such as urine)

Experienced Medical Assistants (clinical tasks)

- ❏ Administer first aid or CPR (cardiopulmonary resuscitation, a set of skills that can revive a person who has stopped breathing or whose heart has stopped)
- ❏ Assist physicians with exams and treatments (sterilize equipment and hand doctor instruments)
- ❏ Perform certain diagnostic tests (take electrocardiograms, for instance, to record the heartbeat to check

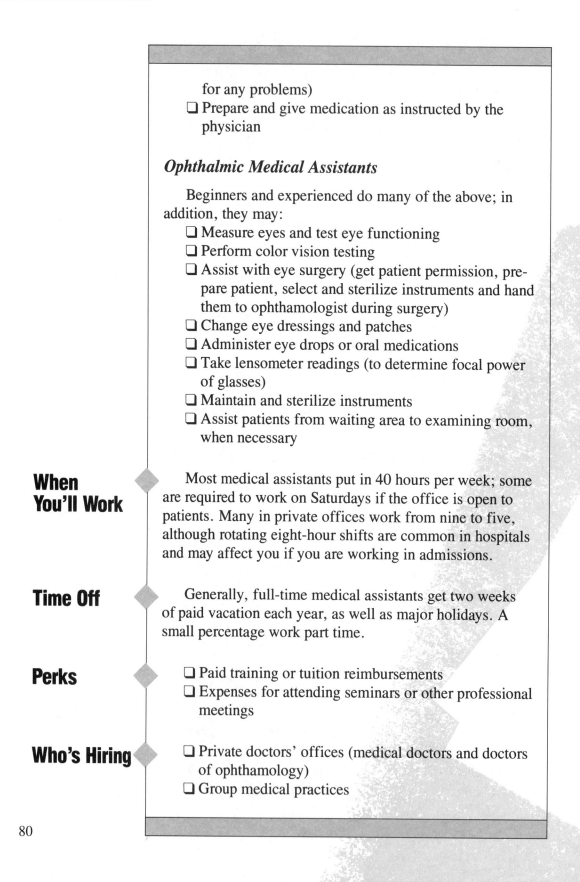

for any problems)
- ❏ Prepare and give medication as instructed by the physician

Ophthalmic Medical Assistants

Beginners and experienced do many of the above; in addition, they may:
- ❏ Measure eyes and test eye functioning
- ❏ Perform color vision testing
- ❏ Assist with eye surgery (get patient permission, prepare patient, select and sterilize instruments and hand them to ophthamologist during surgery)
- ❏ Change eye dressings and patches
- ❏ Administer eye drops or oral medications
- ❏ Take lensometer readings (to determine focal power of glasses)
- ❏ Maintain and sterilize instruments
- ❏ Assist patients from waiting area to examining room, when necessary

When You'll Work

Most medical assistants put in 40 hours per week; some are required to work on Saturdays if the office is open to patients. Many in private offices work from nine to five, although rotating eight-hour shifts are common in hospitals and may affect you if you are working in admissions.

Time Off

Generally, full-time medical assistants get two weeks of paid vacation each year, as well as major holidays. A small percentage work part time.

Perks

- ❏ Paid training or tuition reimbursements
- ❏ Expenses for attending seminars or other professional meetings

Who's Hiring

- ❏ Private doctors' offices (medical doctors and doctors of ophthamology)
- ❏ Group medical practices

❏ Public and private medical clinics
❏ Hospitals
❏ Offices of other health practitioners

❏ Exposure to infectious blood, bodily fluid or airborne viruses and diseases (it's essential to follow safety precautions)

◆ **On-the-Job Hazards**

Beginners and experienced medical assistants: little potential for travel
The only time you may get paid to work outside the office is if you attend a conference, educational seminar or other professional meeting.

◆ **Places You'll Go**

The appearance of private doctor's offices, group practices and clinics ranges from simple to elegant—much depends on the style and taste of the doctor or doctors who own it and the type of patients they hope to attract. Public clinics that are new facilities are likely to offer a more pleasant work environment than those that have been around for some time and may not get the funding to redecorate. Medical assistants who work in hospitals often work in officelike environments away from the hubbub of the hospital, unless they are working at an admissions desk.

◆ **Surroundings**

What you earn depends on your training and experience and often on how well recognized medical assisting is in your area. Average starting salaries are between $13,500 and $14,500 per year. After five to seven years a top earner may make $30,000 to $35,000 per year. In general, salaries vary according to the cost of living in each area.

◆ **Dollars and Cents**

Some medical assistants stay in the profession for a long time, building their skills and moving on to more complicated and demanding procedures until they become office managers. But medical assistants who enjoy the clinical aspect of the work often go back to school for more training

◆ **Moving Up**

to become registered nurses, medical technicians, radiologic technicians or physicians' assistants—all fields that require further education.

Where the Jobs Are

While a great need for medical assistants exists throughout the country, there are more jobs in states where the profession is well known and recognized, such as North Carolina and Florida.

School Information

One- and two-year medical assisting programs are offered by profit-making vocational schools and by community colleges. (Some nonaccredited programs may take as little as two or three months to complete.)

One-year programs generally result in a certificate of completion. Two-year programs at community colleges can result in an associate degree in medical assisting or an associate degree in technical arts, science or applied arts, with the major program emphasis being medical assisting.

Program costs vary; the least expensive are community colleges, where tuition can be as little as $200 a year to as much as $1,000 a year. Some for-profit schools charge as much as $3,000 to $6,800 per year.

Two major educational accrediting bodies, the Committee on Allied Health Education and Accreditation (CAHEA) and the Accrediting Bureau of Health Education Schools (ABHES), evaluate educational programs. The advantage of completing a CAHEA- or ABHES-accredited program is that they prepare you to take a competency exam. If you pass the CAHEA exam, you can call yourself a certified medical assistant or CMA (recognition awarded by the American Association of Medical Assistants, one of the two major professional organizations for medical assistants). If you pass the ABHES exam, you can call yourself a registered medical assistant (recognition awarded by American Medical Technologists, the other major national professional association).

If you haven't completed a CAHEA- or ABHES-accredited program, you can take either of their exams once you have a year of work experience under your belt. The advantage of becoming a certified or registered medical assistant is that you are more marketable; some doctors see approved training as an extra protection against malpractice suits.

Finally, the Joint Review Committee of Ophthalmic Medical Personnel (JRCOMP) approves six-month- to one-year ophthalmic medical assistant programs. Once you complete such a program, you are eligible to take the certifying exam developed and administered by the Joint Commission on Allied Health Personnel in Ophthamology. If you do not attend a JRCOMP-approved program, you can become eligible to take the exam by completing the home study course developed and published by the American Academy of Ophthamology and by working one year as an ophthalmic medical assistant.

While the field is open to men and women, 95 percent of all medical assistants are women.

The Male/Female Equation

The Bad News
❑ Low pay
❑ Risk of exposure to infectious viruses and diseases
❑ Having to deal with difficult patients

The Good News
❑ Plenty of jobs
❑ Work hours more like the business world than the medical world
❑ Opportunities for on-the-job training

Making Your Decision: What to Consider

American Association of Medical Assistants (AAMA)
20 North Wacker Drive
Suite 1575
Chicago, Illinois 60606
800-228-2262 or 312-899-1500

You can find out which schools in your area offer CAHEA-accredited programs by writing or calling this organization.

More Information Please

American Medical Technologists, Registered Medical Assistants (AMT)
710 Higgins Road
Park Ridge, Illinois 60068
708-823-5169

Write for information about career opportunities and requirements for becoming a registered medical assistant.

Accrediting Bureau of Health Education Schools (ABHES)
Oak Manor Office
29089 U.S. 20 West
Elkhart, Indiana 46514
219-293-0124

You can find out which schools in your area offer ABHES-accredited programs by writing or calling this organization.

Joint Commission on Allied Health Personnel in Ophthamology
2025 Woodlane Drive
St. Paul, Minnesota 55125-2995
612-731-2944

You can get information about career opportunities, education programs and requirements to take a certifying exam by writing or calling this organization.

WHAT IT'S REALLY LIKE

Jody Magruder, 24,
certified medical assistant,
Gig Harbor, Washington
Years in the job: two as a CMA, eight as an
uncertified medical assistant

What do you currently do?

I'm a medical assistant with many responsibilities in an
extremely fast-paced office. My physician sees between 40
and 50 patients a day, which is good because I like to keep
busy. In the mornings I turn on the lights and equipment
and get my lab work set up, which involves laying out tubes
and needle sizes, sterilizing equipment and checking supplies. Then I call the patients in from the waiting room and
take weights, blood pressures and get information on why
they've come. If it's for a complete physical, I draw blood,
run their urinalysis, do an EKG (electrocardiogram), set up
for the PAP smears for female patients and do blood stool
testing.

When my doctor is examining a female patient, I'll often
stay in the room to assist him or to make the patient feel
more comfortable. In my free time I call in prescriptions

85

and pull the charts and ledgers for the next day. I'm also responsible for all of the filing and assist with some of the typing, making appointments and answering the phone. I work from 9:00 A.M. until 5:30 P.M., or until the last patient is in the examining room.

Where is your office?

I work in a family practice just seven miles from my home, which is in Gig Harbor, Washington. The practice is about 20 miles from a hospital and 10 miles from an urgent care center. We see a lot of injuries—labor and industry and motor vehicle accident cases. We don't do X-rays or deal with broken bones or lacerations; for those, patients go to the emergency room.

How did you get started as a medical assistant?

Ten years ago I started working part time for an optometrist while I was still in high school and decided I wanted to get more into surgery. I found a job with a podiatrist who trained me to assist with surgeries. I would do such things as chemically sterilize a patient's foot, hand the doctor instruments, change dressings, help with the cleanup. It turned out that the woman I replaced was going to school to become a medical assistant. After nine months I, too, stopped working for the podiatrist and went to school to become a medical assistant. I decided I wanted to learn terminology and also about medications and basic science, because I felt I was inadequately trained in these areas. I entered a one-year program at Portland Community College, graduated with an associate degree in 1990 and worked in Oregon for Kaiser Permanente (a health maintenance organization), primarily in pediatrics (the care of children).

What do you like most about your job?

I enjoy working with patients and doing the hands-on medical procedures—drawing blood, lancing cysts and packing wounds.

What do you like least?

The front office work. I don't really care to deal with the insurance companies, especially having to explain all the changes in Medicare rules over and over to unhappy patients 15 times a day.

What was the hardest part of being a medical assistant during the first few years?

I didn't have a problem doing any of the medical stuff—drawing blood or lancing cysts. What was hard was trying to communicate effectively to patients, because we don't get much training in it. It's very important to try to explain to them what they need to know and have them retain it because of malpractice these days.

What do you plan to be doing in five years?

I'd like to continue with my education and get a bachelor's degree. I'm interested in translating doctor's notes for malpractice attorneys and want to see if they'd consider using medical assistants. It's different than the office setting, which I've been in for a long time. I'd also like to teach.

What advice can you give someone thinking of becoming a medical assistant?

Education is tremendously important. I encourage certification and active enrollment and participation in your professional organization. Even doctors don't always know the difference between a certified medical assistant and a medical assistant—and they should, since they need to be a little more careful about who they choose to work for them. A lot of people don't know about this profession. They often confuse us with nurses.

Nina Bagley, 37,
office manager/certified medical
assistant for a one-doctor office,
Fayetteville, North Carolina
Years in the job: 18

What do you currently do?

I'm a certified medical assistant who works as an office manager for a specialty practice in ophthalmology. I'm involved in both the administrative and clinical aspects of medical assisting—answering the phone, scheduling patient appointments, as well as surgery, doing insurance billing and the back office procedures of patient care. I work from 8:30 A.M. to 5:30 P.M. four days per week.

How did you get started as a medical assistant?
I didn't originally choose a medical profession. My real
interest was in figures—bookkeeping, accounting, that type
of thing. I left college after one year and needed a job.
There was an opening in the medical complex where one
of my girlfriends worked, so I wound up working for a
doctor there. Soon I became interested in what I was doing
and decided to return to school and get certified as a medical assistant. The doctor paid for my certification exam;
he's also paid for all my continuing education since that
time, to keep my certification valid, as well as for any other
courses that help me in my profession. I've been working
for this same doctor now for 18 years.

Medical assisting has changed so much in the past five to
six years that I've had to go back and learn new procedures.
For instance, when I first started, insurance coding was
optional—now it's mandatory. Since it's been constant
change and relearning, I'm doing a lot more than I did 18
years ago, and I haven't had time to get bored.

Now I do some accounting, payroll and a lot more instruc-
tional counseling with patients, explaining why they have
to take different medications, what type of surgery they're
going to have. Because there are only a certain number of
procedures to learn in ophthalmology, I have time to learn
other things, such as how to test visual field analysis with
special machines. Because my physician does flight physi-
cals for the Federal Aviation Administration, I can now do
electronic EKG transmissions on my own, as well as urinalysis, which I normally wouldn't do. That has kept me interested. Plus, the office is very fast paced; my doctor alone
sees anywhere from 40 to 50 patients per day.

**How long did it take you to feel established as a medical
assistant?**
It took 12 years. I think there's so much to learn in a medical office that it's overwhelming. If you aren't a person
who can do more than one job at a time, you can't function
in a doctor's office—you have to learn to do two or three
things well at once. It's just within the past six years that
I've felt very accomplished.

What was the hardest part of being a medical assistant during the first few years?
Getting over feeling intimidated by the physicians. I didn't have a lot of self-confidence, and it took me a long time to learn that they didn't know everything even though they're better educated than me. A lot of young people are real hesitant; they're afraid if they ask stupid questions or do something wrong, they'll get jumped on. But that's not the case. It's not that people don't want to explain things to you—sometimes they just don't have the time.

What do you like most about your job?
I enjoy building a rapport and having contact with my patients. The physician I work for isn't a real talker. I make myself learn a lot of extra things so I can fill in all the questions patients ask that he hasn't answered. I like educating them and explaining about medication, and learning about diseases so I can answer their questions.

What do you like least?
The phone is my number one enemy. It brings me the most stress and is a constant interruption.

What are you most proud of?
Learning how to speak out, how to take charge and be the authority. I'm very confident in my area of expertise. I've learned how to get my point across in a friendly way, how to handle a lot of the situations you encounter when dealing with people, including disagreements. You really have to be a people person to be in the medical profession.

What do you expect to be doing in five years?
I plan to go back to school for business administration and eventually go into a large medical complex and be the comptroller (the chief accountant). Although I'm sure I'll miss working with patients and may find myself going back to pursue the clinical end at some later date, I want to try focusing on the administrative side and get formal training in some of the things I do already. It's possible that I'll go for my RN so I'll have the option of getting into the clinical end, but I really don't picture myself in a hospital setting taking care of patients.

What advice can you give someone thinking of going into this field?

Learn as much about the international classification of diseases and the coding and procedures for insurance, because that is the focus of the future in medical practice. Unfortunately, a lot of the medical assisting programs aren't really teaching such things. Get certified—certification gives you book knowledge of everything that goes on in a doctor's office and helps you to answer patients' questions and keep their confidence.

Medical assisting is a wonderful career for someone coming out of high school. You can get a job in a physician's office and decide whether you want to be up front in the paper-pushing insurance end and do the receptionist thing with the patients—or whether you want to get in the back and learn to take blood pressures and draw blood. If you work in a small office, you can try out all areas and grow in the one you choose. Lots of times, if the physician finds you're working well in that area, he'll let you take off and really go.

Kimberly Towlson, 21,
medical secretary/medical assistant, Ware, Massachusetts
Years in the job: 10 months as a full-time medical secretary, three years as a part-time one

What do you currently do?

I'm a medical secretary in a neurosurgeon's office, though I'm not a certified medical assistant. I focus on administration, not on clinical things like taking blood. Though I'm supposed to start work at 8:45 A.M., I'm usually there at 8:00 to make sure everything is ready, such as getting the patients' charts in order, turning on the lights and the computer. Later, I bring patients into the examining room, do some billing, transcribe the doctor's progress notes from a tape, answer the phone and book surgeries on the computer.

On days when my physician is in surgery and there aren't

patients in the office, I call patients about scheduling and answer their questions. When the doctor is examining women patients, I stand in the examining room with them so they feel more comfortable.

How did you get started as a medical assistant?
I was studying accounting in college until I got a part-time job working in a medical office and then decided to switch my major. I went to Springfield Technical Community College for my associate degree in medical office administration and also continued working in the medical office for three years—answering phones, doing data entry on a computer and making appointments.

What do you like most about your job?
I like learning something every day. I enjoy going into the room and watching an exam. If you're interested, the doctor will explain things to you. I find it amazing that by doing an exam he can tell what's wrong. I used to work in pediatrics, where the most you'd see is a cold or pneumonia. But when you work for a neurosurgeon, you see brain tumors, as well as a million back and neck problems. I learn a little bit more each day.

What do you like least?
Dealing with difficult patients. In school you're taught as much as possible about dealing with patients, but until you actually get into a confrontation with them, you don't really know what it's like.

What are you most proud of?
It feels good when a patient calls me after a doctor's visit to ask questions and I can help them feel less nervous and more comfortable going into surgery.

What advice can you give someone considering a career as a medical assistant?
To be successful in this job you need a lot of patience. An internship or part-time work is a good way to get experience and decide whether medical assisting is something you really want to do.

WILL YOU FIT INTO THE WORLD OF HEALTH CARE?

Before you enroll in a training program or start to search for a job in one of the careers described in this book, it's smart to figure out whether that career is a good fit, given your background, skills and personality. There are a number of ways to do that. They include:

❑ Talk to people who work in the field. Find out what they like and don't like about their jobs, what kinds of people their employers hire and what their recommendations are about training.

❑ Use a computer to help you identify career options. Some of the most widely used programs are "Discover," by the American College Testing Service, "SIGI Plus," developed by the Educational Testing Service, and "Career Options," by Peterson's. Some public libraries make this career software available to library users at low or no cost. The career-counseling or guidance offices of your high school or local community college are other possibilities.

❑ Take a vocational interest test. The most commonly used ones are the Strong-Campbell Interest Inventory and the Kuder Occupational Interest Survey. High schools and colleges usually offer free testing to their students and alumni through their guidance and career planning offices. Many career counselors in private practice or at community job centers are also trained to interpret results.

❑ Talk to a career counselor. You can find one by asking friends and colleagues if they know of any good ones. Or contact the career information office of the adult education division of a local college. Their staff and workshop leaders often do one-on-one counseling. The job information services division of major libraries sometimes offer low- or no-cost counseling by appointment. Or check the *Yellow Pages* under "Vocational Guidance."

Before you spend time, energy or money doing any of the above, take one or more of the following five quizzes (one for each career described in the book). The results can help you confirm whether you really are cut out to work in a particular career.

If the job of nursing assistant interests you, take this quiz:

Read each statement, then choose 0, 5 or 10. The rating scale below explains what each number means.

> **0** = Disagree
> **5** = Agree somewhat
> **10** = Strongly agree

____I have good spelling skills and can write down information with ease

____I can clearly communicate information to others with whom I work, without feeling intimidated because they have more education

____I could feed patients who may have difficulty chewing and swallowing food

____I am healthy and have good upper-body strength

____I have a clean, neat personal appearance and good hygiene

____I am patient and tolerant and can handle demanding or odd behavior of people who are confused, disoriented or sick

____I can stand working on my feet for long hours

____I don't need other people's recognition to take pride in my work

___I would not feel embarrassed helping people with intimate bodily functions, such as going to the bathroom

___I have empathy for those who are very sick and old but can remain detached enough so that I do not get depressed

Now add up your score.   ___Total points

If your total points were less than 50, you probably do not have sufficient interest or inclination to learn what's required to become a nursing assistant. If your total points were between 50 and 75, you may have what it takes to get into the field, but be sure to do more investigation by following the suggestions earlier in this section. If your total points were 75 or more, it's highly likely that you are a good candidate to work as a nursing assistant.

If the job of home health aide interests you, take this quiz:

Read each statement, then choose 0, 5 or 10. The rating scale below explains what each number means.

$$0 = \text{Disagree}$$
$$5 = \text{Agree somewhat}$$
$$10 = \text{Strongly agree}$$

___I have a friendly personality and a cheerful, positive attitude

___I would get great satisfaction from helping those who cannot care for themselves

___I am independent and feel comfortable adapting to new situations on a regular basis, such as visiting people's homes

___I have the patience to deal with people who are angry, grumpy or unappreciative of my efforts

___I like to cook and know or am interested in learning more about nutrition and how to prepare special meals for people with particular health needs

___I take pride in housekeeping tasks

___I can get people to talk to me about themselves and
their problems

___I am a good observer and feel I could detect changes in
a patient's condition

___I know the basics of good hygiene and cleanliness

___I am physically strong and able to bend and lift

Now add up your score.   ___Total points

If your total points were less than 50, you probably do
not have sufficient interest or inclination to learn what's
required to become a home health aide. If your total points
were between 50 and 75, you may have what it takes to
become a home health aide, but be sure to do more investigation by following the suggestions earlier in this section.
If your total points were 75 or more, it's highly likely that
you are a good candidate to work as a home health aide.

If you are interested in becoming a licensed practical nurse, take this quiz:

Read each statement, then choose 0, 5 or 10. The rating
scale below explains what each number means.

> **0** = Disagree
> **5** = Agree somewhat
> **10** = Strongly agree

___I have compassion for the sick or injured

___I have excellent powers of observation and would notice
slight differences in a patient's condition

___I don't mind the sight of blood or doing medical proce-
dures such as changing bandages and giving injections

___I can respond calmly in an emergency

___I appreciate a clean and orderly environment and don't
mind pitching in to keep it that way

___I have the self-esteem to work under people with more
education and training than me

___I am healthy, with no back problems

___I am interested in learning about biology, anatomy,

pharmacology and nutrition

___I can stand working on my feet for long hours

___I don't need other people's recognition to take pride in my work

Now add up your score.   ___Total points

If your total points were less than 50, you probably do not have sufficient interest or inclination to learn what's required to become a licensed practical nurse. If your total points were between 50 and 75, you may have what it takes to get into licensed practical nursing, but be sure to do more investigation by following the suggestions earlier in this section. If your total points were 75 or more, it's highly likely that you are a good candidate to work in the field of licensed practical nursing.

If becoming a radiologic technologist interests you, take this quiz:

Read each statement, then choose 0, 5 or 10. The rating scale below explains what each number means.

> **0** = Disagree
> **5** = Agree somewhat
> **10** = Strongly agree

___I have good manual dexterity (I have nimble fingers and have no trouble using them on tasks that require precise movements)

___I am physically strong and have good upper-body strength

___I don't mind being on my feet a lot

___I am self-confident and would feel comfortable working with people who have more education than I do

___I like the idea of helping those who are sick or injured

___I am detail oriented and organized

___I enjoy working with computers and like the idea of operating high-tech equipment

___I enjoy and do well in math and science subjects

___I get along easily and communicate well with other people and enjoy working as part of a team

___I don't mind the sight of blood and I stay calm in emergencies

Now add up your score.   ___Total points

If your total points were less than 50, you probably do not have sufficient interest or inclination to learn what's required to become a radiologic technologist. If your total points were between 50 and 75, you may have what it takes to get into radiologic technology, but be sure to do more investigation by following the suggestions earlier in this section. If your total points were 75 or more, it's highly likely that you are a good candidate to work in the field of radiologic technology.

If becoming a medical assistant interests you, take this quiz:

Read each statement, then choose 0, 5 or 10. The rating scale below explains what each number means.

0 = Disagree
5 = Agree somewhat
10 = Strongly agree

___I can clearly communicate instructions and information

___I have a friendly personality

___I have no problem respecting someone's privacy

___I am organized and can manage several tasks at a time

___I enjoy doing clerical tasks such as typing, answering phones, filing and using office equipment

___I am patient and don't mind repeating the same instructions or information frequently

___I am able to handle difficult people and don't get ruffled when people get upset

___I don't need other people's recognition to take pride in my work

___I can stay calm in emergencies

___I am not squeamish about blood or the thought of doing simple medical procedures such as giving injections or taking blood

Now add up your score.   ___Total points

If your total points were less than 50, you probably do not have sufficient interest or inclination to learn what's required to become a medical assistant. If your total points were between 50 and 75, you may have what it takes to get into medical assisting, but be sure to do more investigation by following the suggestions earlier in this section. If your total points were 75 or more, it's highly likely that you are a good candidate to work in the field of medical assisting.

ABOUT THE AUTHORS

Susan Gordon is a freelance writer in Los Angeles. She has written on health, fitness and cultural affairs for *McCalls, Longevity, Self, The Los Angeles Times, L.A. Style* and *Metropolitan Home.* She has worked on staff as a writer and editor for *Glamour, Seventeen, Woman's Day* and *California* magazines.

Kristin Hohenadel is a Los Angeles-based writer and editor who has worked on staff at *L. A. Weekly* and *California.* She teaches journalism at the University of Redlands in California.